Shul

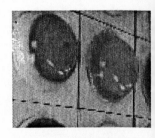

THREE RIVERS PRESS
NEW YORK

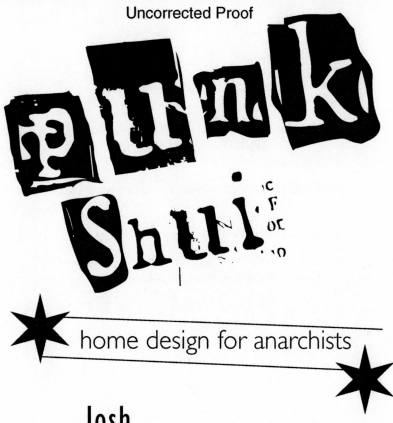

Punk Shui

home design for anarchists

Josh
Amatore Hughes

Published in the United States by Three Rivers Press, an imprint of the Crown Publishing Group, a division of Random House, Inc., New York.
www.crownpublishing.com

Three Rivers Press and the Tugboat design are registered trademarks of Random
House, Inc.

Library of Congress Cataloging-in-Publication Data

Hughes, Josh Amatore.
    Punk shui : home design for anarchists / Josh Amatore Hughes.— 1st ed.
        p. cm.
    1. Interior decoration—Psychological aspects.   2. Interior decoration—Humor.
    I. Title.
    NK2113.H84 2006
    747—dc22   2005024222

ISBN-13: 978-0-307-23762-0
ISBN-10: 0-307-23762-1
Printed in the United States of America
Design by Sarah Maya Gubkin
10 9 8 7 6 5 4 3 2 1
First Edition

To Sara Beth

contents

intro manifesto

The world can be a pretty unwelcoming place. Oh, it's the daily grind that makes up the fabric of our days, with its coma-inducing traffic jams, four-dollar cups of coffee, the monotone drone of superficial discourse that passes for conversation these days, and the constant commercial assaults on our senses. And it's not limited to the city. Maybe that's where it's the most obvious, but the suburbs can give you something to bitch about, too. The prefab homes, the lookalike cul-de-sacs, the manicured lawns, the strip malls... it's all less than inspiring. As a society, we have stopped making original choices and often operate in an unconscious, droidlike mode as we are fed commercial aesthetic orders through daily subliminal channels.

But this book aims to change all that. No longer will you be the typical consumer. No longer will you be beaten down by the chaos, the stress, the grind, be told how to live or how to design your home and your life. You'll stop doing really predictable things, shopping at places you know are embarrassing, imitating people with whom you have nothing in common, and, in general, living a lie. You will become a more creative and interesting version of yourself, and your home will become a haven for expressing this creativity, this chaos, and this new lifestyle.

We, the proponents of punk shui, believe that as human beings we have the right, the absolute unconditional right, to feel inspired, free, and alive in our homes and beyond. This basic belief embraces an assortment of things typically condemned by "Them." The punk shui aesthetic welcomes no-nos like bashing, trashing, destroying, maiming, mutilating, battering, or remaking, rethinking, reimagining, and doing bold creative and/or destructive things to that which is typically sacred in the world of home and lifestyle design as we know it. Walls no longer contain us; boundaries disappear and are replaced with a pulsing energy that fuels creative freedom. By partaking in this movement, we express our absolute freedom and disregard for authority (design, societal or otherwise) and basically make an effort to do whatever the hell we want. Damn, it feels good.

There is a revolution happening in home design that inevitably leads to lifestyle design. No longer does the "norm" duplicate the lives of those who seek a punk-ass lifestyle. No longer will you follow the masses. Destroying furniture, reconfiguring rooms, and totally renovating a home in a completely untraditional way can transform life and the principles on which society depends. That, my friends, is what punk shui is about. I invite you to partake, and remake your world with this concept.

Through punk shui I am going to show you how to survive the chaotic, unpredictable world outside and embrace the freakishness that so many believe (in vain) that they can control. If you follow my example, you'll retain a little bit of creativity, originality and sense of self through rebelling, tearing shit up and going against the grain. And, you'll be a lot more interesting.

1

the Punk Shui way

Let's Talk About Me

My name is Josh, and I'm the originator of punk shui. Inspired by the large number of crappy designers that fuel our mucked-up cultural aesthetic, I have devoted myself to helping those who desire more from life and their living space, seeking to push the limits of what people consider "design." I'm based in New York City, but I have clients all over the country. I own a company that specializes in advising punk shui worshipers how to do as I do. I design "interiors," but I also do sculpture, installations, and film that tend to reflect the punk shui aesthetic. Basically, I help a lot of my clients to embrace chaos, to break the rules, and to let some original ideas out of the box. Through the concept of punk shui, I work to further the general belief that individual freedom should prevail, and the design equivalent of Ashley Simpson should *not*.

We've had quite the wave of new punk shui followers recently. Most are people who are sick of doing things in a predictable, boring way and want to shake up their lives. A lot of them are artists, and some are people who have always wanted to be artists. In general, they are people sick of following the pack and doing what all of their friends deem "cool" or "acceptable." Whatever the case, there's no prerequisite to punk shui'ing your place—only this: you must be open-minded, ready for the ride, and not easily offended.

Check It

Let's go over a few things to see if you're the kind of person who is a candidate for punk shui. You should rethink your boring design aesthetic if you've ever

* fought the lingering distaste that accompanies "cleaning up" your apartment or office
* felt a nasty malaise when confronted with art or furniture options in any chain store or national retailer
* dreaded having someone over because you thought they were an obsessive neat freak and would look down their nose at your less-than-IKEAfied apartment
* just wanted to shred *Martha Stewart Living* with a chain saw or destroy a display in Target because, well, look at it...
* felt you want to create something unique, a true aesthetic all your own, but have never considered yourself

the type of person who would go through the trouble of actually "decorating" your living space, or, god forbid, try your hand at art collecting or conceiving

*   felt envious when walking into a sibling's or roommate's   garbage-and-dirty-clothes/dishes-in-the-sink-infested living space

*   watched an episode of *Friends* and then had to lock your bottle of Valium in the bottom of your special pillbox so you wouldn't be tempted to maybe down the entire thing in a sudden suicidal frenzy

and finally...

*   Do you like books with grainy pictures of broken furniture?

*   Do you look this good in pictures?

If you answered yes to any of these questions, get it on with punk shui. In this book I will tell you how. It's not just about decorating your space, it's about embracing a different lifestyle—one that transforms your habits, style, and mindset.

Forget Everything You Know

It's time to stop posing and pretending when it comes the atmosphere that surrounds you. You can do it. Wipe off that facial expression you learned and replace it with something you actually mean. Act like you feel and feel like you act. You owe it to yourself. You owe it to me.

You're going to have to let go of everything you've learned about home decoration, paying attention to different styles, looks, and what others think. In order to live a punk shui life, you have to let go of any preconceptions you have about what your living space is "supposed" to be like.

Fear-Based BS

Fear is paralyzed joy.
—Timothy Speed Levitch, author of *Speedology*

What exactly are your afraid of? Are you afraid of not enjoying what you do for a living? Afraid of not finding anyone who understands you? Afraid of not understanding yourself? Afraid of becoming a complete square? Afraid of ending up like your parents? Whatever your bullshit is, it's bullshit. In this book, I'm going to help you get rid of any fear-based hesitation, insecurity, or any other hurdles that keep you from punking out your space so that it is a place you'd truly *live* in.

This doesn't have to do with acting like anyone of whom you might have been in awe; it has to do with living by the same tenets as the truly original and creative. I'll state the obvious again (because even though it's obvious, for many it doesn't seem to stick): You don't need fame, an impressive career, the right hairstyle, or even money in order to embrace the essence of punk shui. This isn't some obnoxious "trend" that was started by a celebrity or by a purveyor of commercial trends like Urban Outfitters or MTV; this is just me persuading you to let yourself out of the box. It's people who, like you, are sick of following the crowd, of running a hamster wheel, of dwelling in predictability. It's people like you who have decided that they can't be categorized, and may actually enjoy heavy machinery, destruction, and general weirdness.

What's that cliché, "home is where the heart is"? Well, I say, "home is where the art is"—or, hell, "home is where the party is."

That's true when you bash a hole in your wall, saw your recliner in half, or try your hand at sculpture. Punk shui is about developing your own aesthetic that may be inspired by others, but is never owned by anyone. Throughout this book, we'll be

* recognizing, identifying, and dismantling the design traditions that work against the "you" that you give a shit about
* getting over what other people think
* accepting the nihilistic living space
* figuring out what your personal punk shui style is, room by room
* rethinking or completely trashing general living space assumptions
* checking out some innovative stuff my clients have done
* meeting some people who have made their way in the world with punk shui
* and, of course, having a damn good time

A Few Notes on Your Mom's Design Aesthetic

You know the kind of people who do feng shui. I can't resist saying something about them here. If you're putting chimes in your doorway to ward off evil spirits and you're color-coding your bedroom to signify the womb and rebirth, then you're probably someone Courtney Love might enjoy collecting crystals with, and you should put this book down and back slowly away. Feng shui is used to control energy (*ch'i*). Bad ch'i is to be avoided and good ch'i is supposed to make you feel all happy and smiley. In punk shui, you must accept all energy, regardless of whether it makes you feel trapped, sick to your stomach, sexually aroused, as if you might be hallucinating, or as if you're afraid to go to sleep. In fact, if it screws with you, all the better; I never said this would be painless.

Feng shui (pronounced "fung shway") is the ancient mystical art of Chinese geomancy, the terrestrial equivalent of astrology, studying the dynamic relationship between humans and the surrounding environment. *Feng* means "wind" and *shui* means "water." Feng shui is the study of ch'i in our environment. In short, it is not even close to being as exciting or life-altering as punk shui.

Punk shui (pronounced "punk shway") is the ancient art of urban survival, the terrestrial equivalent of chaos. It is much revered in underground subcultures and within the bedrooms of teenagers, artists, and the basic subculture minority, but until now it has not reached the outer limits of "acceptability." Whatever. That's about to change. In short, punk shui is the practice of creating a chaos in the home so deafening that it creates a contrast in life powerful enough to enable you to cope with the inevitable shit sandwich that is the outside world.

So there it is. Forget creating some type of "safe haven" called home. Why would you want to create an illusion of comfort when you're just going to be disappointed as soon as you step outside? Finally, after years of trying it "their way," I stumbled on an idea so utterly pure and foolproof that even Steve Jobs is jealous. Punk shui is not just a design concept, but a coping mechanism so powerful you'll be able to ditch those 500 milligrams of Vicodin you've been washing down with your morning latte.

The Weirdos

As Mike Watt, bassist, spielmeister/indie-punk rock godfather, said, when I discussed the punk shui aesthetic with him, "Punk was an excuse to get all of the weirdos together." Well, that's what we'll be doing in this book. We're going to get the weirdos together and talk about how they get inspired.

Punk shui doesn't rely solely on the existence of feng shui, and it doesn't rely on the preexistence of actual punk music. Punk shui is about the art that emerges when no rules apply. It is not about hanging up a bunch of punk posters and decorating your living room as a shrine to Johnny Thunders. Wouldn't it be lame if it were that simple?

Step into the PS Zone

I'm sure you know what nihilism, irrationality, and anarchy mean (or you think you do.) You may have even studied these concepts in some BS classroom. But have you really discovered them? Have you imagined them as they apply to your pathetic little routine existence? Have you considered that their real meanings, if taken to heart, could have a completely amazing effect on your freedom, your creativity, and even your sex life?

Through bashing you will remove the brainwash; you will be energized as you take a second look at the decisions you made when you designed the environment where you live. You have to do it before you are permanently lulled into a noncreative, zombielike state by prepackaged ideas. By reexamining why you do what you do, and by thinking about how to ignite some type of fire in your mundane, everyday rigmarole you will begin to free your mind and free your pad.

When you practice punk shui, you're taking a step toward being a nonconformist in our society. Boycott these obnoxious, corporate stores like IKEA, Pottery Barn, Bed Bath and Beyond, and Target. These stores take away our creative and artistic choices. Let's face it. When you and twelve of your friends have the same end table in your apartments, because you all hit the same crappy sale, you feel like a douchebag.

Anarchist

This is a rocket launcher, aka "The Law." And yes, it is real.

ANARCHY ('a-ner-ké', medieval Latin, *anarchia,* from Greek *anarchos,* having no ruler): the absence or denial of any authority or established order; DISORDER

Okay, there's a lot of room here to interpret, but basically I want you to be an anarchist in your own living space. You don't need rules, you don't need to adhere to the "authority," whether it's your mom, *Wallpaper* magazine, or your boy/girlfriend. You don't have to have to do anything according to anyone, anywhere, anyhow. From now on, it's about adhering to the wild anarchy of your own nature—not the manicured BS of the rest of the design world. Got it?

Celebrate it. Go ahead and do something right now that feels a little nuts. Turn a table upside down, go outside without your pants on, build a shrine in your kitchen to your favorite band. Take the first step in a journey that will lead you where you've never been before. After you take that step, you're going to feel pretty awesome. Unless you do something to piss someone off, in which case you will get a nice little hit of adrenaline. That can be good, too.

Employ the philosophy of anarchy to your design, and if you're lucky, it will trickle into your lifestyle, that shitty job you go to every day, and assist you in flipping off all of the assholes who give you orders.

Punk Shui Don'ts

I know I said no rules, but we do have a few "suggestions" for you. Before we begin remaking your pad, I'll give you an idea of things that I don't recommend for your aesthetic sphere (unless they are used the in least earnest way—but we'll cover that loophole later). Rob Lanham, author of *Food Court Druids, Cherohonkees and Other Creatures Unique to the Republic* and *The Hipster Handbook,* helped me come up with this short list of things to avoid:

* anything inspired by *Southern Living* or *Good House-keeping* catalogs
* plate collections for the wall
* anything your well-meaning mom, aunt, or older neighbor bought you for a housewarming present
* the design technique you copied from a reality home-design show
* any sponge-paint project you or your living mate put on a wall

* flowery or Victorian themes (any theme, as we'll say a few times in this book, sucks)
* animal-inspired motifs: "I have family members who are obsessed with cats, bunny rabbits, ducks, or geese. If you ever make a proclamation about a particular fondness for a pet, you're doomed, because you will get animal-inspired presents from that point on," Rob advised.
* ceramic figurine collection (unless you've got some broken pieces)
* the frat or sorority roommate (Rob recalled, "When I was in college, I got stuck with this roommate who transformed my apartment into the cheesiest frat-boy pad you've very seen. He put up a Camaro poster. Everything this guy owned, he bought through Marlboro Miles or Camel Cash. I was in frat-boy hell.")

Warped Aesthetics

Now that we've gone over what *not* to do (believe me, that is not a concept I typically encourage), you need to get a little warped. You might be thinking that you have to rip shit up, punch holes in the wall, destroy furniture, and basically transform your apartment into a total wreck to practice punk shui. Pretty much, yes. That is the preferred way to do it.

2

Getting Started

Implements of Destruction

Let's get you outfitted with the proper punk shui tools. Axes, chain saws, blowtorches, and other formal tools of destruction are recommended for heavy work. I've also found I can do a whole lot with a baseball bat. Anything that's capable of breaking something else is a great tool. At this point you should reinvent your idea of tools in general. Any-

An ax is a great old-school tool for remodeling some furniture. (Budman's Studio)

thing can be a destructive tool—your rolling pin, a chair leg—the sky's the limit. I suggest a toolkit for redefining some more-intricate sculptures. Screwdrivers and ice picks are useful when making specific small holes in things or taking things apart. Machetes are excellent for nice, clean tears in furniture or wallpaper, or for hacking at curtains.

For the extreme lovers of destruction—the mere presence of tools of destruction can really change a room. Check it.

Firearms can be pretty useful in damaging or "distressing" your things. Don't you love that word? Designers use it when they want some paint rubbed off something. For the purposes of punk shui, I'd like to define "distressing" something as actually *causing it distress,* rather than its popular use, which seems to entail giving it a cutesy makeover for stores like Pottery Barn, where they dab some paint remover here and there over a coat of new paint and mark up the price 400 percent. My handy .38 Special Smith & Wesson does the trick when I want the bullet-hole effect—now that's distress.

Paints and plaster are awesome when you want to create. Don't limit yourself to the paint in the home-decorating section. Find anything that has color pigment: industrial, oil, acrylic paint, even food coloring.

Allow yourself to think creatively as to how you'll apply the paint. You don't have to use a brush to paint walls or objects. Use anything—from clothes to newspaper. Hell, rub paint all over yourself

I used this baby on a few walls and was not disappointed.

and do some bodywork on your floors and walls. You can put paint down the barrel of an air rifle and shoot color everywhere. You can use a paint gun to decorate your whole place.

Use What You've Got

Later in this book we're going to walk through each room and explore its specific punk shui potential. For now, begin to notice what you have. As I said, anything can be considered a tool, and anything can be altered. Do you have an old piece of furniture that's been pissing you off lately? That's a good place to start.

Don't think, just do it. Don't ponder—just plunder.

By using what you've got, you will save money, you'll be more creative, and you'll be pretty damn impressed with yourself. And you won't have that nasty, sinking feeling you get when you receive your credit-card bill in the mail after "redecorating" your apartment.

When you use what you already own or can find on the street, you are giving things a second or third life. One of the basic elements of punk shui is creatively reinventing another life for space and objects. You can change the energy of the object or space by using it for another purpose. As you prepare to punk shui your home, remember that you probably have everything you need right there. There is no need to go out and drop a bunch of cash. Not only does money hinder creativity, in my opinion, but it is also hard to come by if you had the guts to say "screw you" to the norm. The antiestablishment attitude sometimes limits employability (see the "Anarchist" section, page ■■).

Perhaps You Lack Cash

Punk is all about being broke and getting by. As our legendary designer-at-large, Norman Gosney, says, "I saw punk come up in the U.K., and the punk aesthetic is about having no money. Everything's done on the cheap…often it reeks of no taste and no common acceptance of the norm. A vital ingredient of punk is CHEAP, because otherwise you're straying into Martha Stewartism where you buy these things that you want. You must spend very little money. You replace money with talent, ideas and humor."

It's true. We've discussed no common acceptance of the norm by ignoring everything you've been told to do and doing whatever you want.

In Legs McNeil's *Please Kill Me*, Joey Ramone is quoted as saying, "When John found his guitar he didn't have much money—he bought the guitar for fifty dollars." And that was how it was done. When Lou Reed told Johnny Ramone that he wasn't playing "the right kind of guitar," Johnny was pissed. It was what he could afford, and his sound was about nobody else having a Mosrite. That's punk aesthetic at its best.

It's okay to be broke. Embrace broke. After all, we live in a first-world country, and there are plenty of soup kitchens after you've milked, begged, borrowed, and stolen all you can. You've been called a mooch, a slacker, and maybe, with the allowance of a compliment, talented and smart, but at heart a lazy person. Regardless, if you accept your broke-ass, empty bank account, stop bitching, and use what you have or can make to redefine your space, you'll be much better off than if you slave away in a cubicle to make enough money to buy whatever the "hot" designer of the year has declared is *the* thing to have.

And of course, if you happen to be loaded, that's cool, too. But it doesn't mean you have to listen to other people's advice about what looks good and what doesn't.

The Illusion of Taste

The next thing you should assess is your preconceived idea of what some call "taste." This is important, pay attention—*you don't have to have any.* You now have my permission on that very important part of punk shui. In fact, it's completely subjective, this "taste" that famous designers and stores seem to have. Now you must reprogram your brain. I'm going to let you in on a little secret. There is little validity to what people call "good taste." Good taste is like the Easter Bunny and Santa Claus—once you realize that people are inventing for their own comfort, to distract and control others, and because it makes them feel cozy and safe, you realize there is no such thing. Good taste is an illusion, and if you imagine that you will *never* design anything based on anyone else's version of this illusion, you will be one step closer to becoming your own person. And I'll be the first to admit that a disregard for so-called good taste definitely helps a person feel better about being broke.

Your Inner Punk

Okay, this doesn't mean that you need to get some black clothes with plaid patches, snap some spikes around your neck and wrists, and pose as a punk rock fan from the eighties. As I've said before, punk shui is not formed on punk music principles and style. It's its own animal. We adhere to the part of punk that promotes not following rules and doing whatever the hell you want, but you don't have to look the part.

Punk shui is an outlet for your inner rebel. Put yourself back into your mindset at eight years old, when everything you enjoyed doing pissed your mom off. All of that is called for. Play with matches, use your markers and paints on the wall; your "toys" don't have to be in the box, and you can put chewing gum in your friends' hair. As Watt said of punk and creativity, there's something to be said for "seeing the world through a childlike wonder."

What do you really want to do? I mean, seriously. Think about it. Does your furniture in your living room match? Does that make you feel somewhat, well…lame? We hope so. Surely you're not so pa-

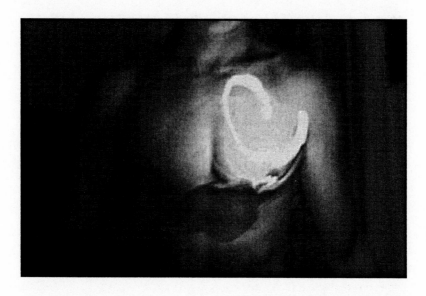

thetic that you would have read this far if it didn't stir some primal restlessness in you to have anything match, or to follow anyone else's sense of style. Even if you have always felt like a bland, vanilla-flavored poser, we assure you that, deep down, you have an inner punk. Wait a sec—this term is not working for me. It sounds too much like "inner child." Let's try that again. Deep down, you probably have some semblance of taste, rebellion, and an artistic sensibility. Right? Well, dig deep to see if you can come up with something remotely interesting and not spoon-fed BS. Pleeeeease. You'll need this sense of personal style in order to move ahead.

3

assess your mess

Assessing Your Digs

Now that you've got that punk inside you thrashing a bit, let's check out your pad. I'm going to bet that something bugs you about where you hang your hat. What is it? Is it the boring, convenient fashion in which the toothpaste is nestled beside the toothbrush—in a toothbrush *holder?* Is it that you actually have the sofa you got at a garage sale (from an old lady who enjoyed large floral patterns) arranged predictably behind a hand-me-down coffee table from your grand-mother? Is it the obnoxious frat letters that hang on the walls because your roommate is an idiot? Is it the paisley printed pillows that your sister gave you for Xmas and you haven't really cared enough to burn—which was your first impulse when you opened the package?

What is it that makes you feel like an uninventive, unimaginative poser and/or square when you bring a date home—or, even worse, when you just come home yourself?

(BTW, we're defining squares and posers as people who are ter-rified to break rules, who give a shit about what other people think. This includes anyone who picked up this book and didn't buy it be-cause they were scared to make a change.)

Prepare Your State of Mind

I'm not going to advocate that you take *illicit drugs,* because we advo-cate choice with punk shui, and now is the time to choose a freer state of mind. You can choose to follow my example, or you can go your own path. I'm certainly not going to tell you to use drugs, but a lot of my clients say that it's easier to get into the process of assessing if your mind has been altered (go figure!). And if you do it, I'd stay away from downers. For those who are into experience-enhancers, stop reading now, go do your thing, then come back and keep reading.

For the other, more boring folk, keep reading but take caution, this may hurt a little. Use your imagination and figure out a way to prepare yourself so that you can look at your apartment through new eyes. What works for you is different for everyone. Find the specific process that will change your perspective from boring, trancelike indifference to being pissed off, wild-eyed, or just a little more adventurous. Maybe it's looking at a photo of your old girlfriend or boyfriend with their new love, or watching a Michael Moore documentary, or going to a favorite bar for an extended amount of time, or a combination of all three. I'll leave that up to you. Whatever it is, do it.

Assess and Make a Mess

Now that you're taking a look at your apartment in a more reckless, unguarded state, notice the difference. Immediately, when you enter your living space, start to take note of anything that sucks, or that makes you feel

* a little too predictable: a hatrack by the door
* that you're doing something your parents taught you: a coffee table in the center of sofas and chairs
* organized: books on a bookshelf (with the spines out), or having all of your CDs and DVDs in the cases in a rack.
* typical: a welcome mat by the door, portraits over the fireplace
* lacking in imagination: you copied your living room décor from a *Wallpaper* magazine

One of my clients, Richard, followed my advice and took a new look at his pad. Of his own volition, he went out and got wasted. He woke up with a one-armed cocktail waitress and a wrecked pickup truck.

Luckily, the wrecked pickup truck was in his living room, so he got a cool punk shui sculpture out of it. I would caution against this approach in the future, though. Drinking and driving is not an activity punk shui endorses.

Annihilating the Pattern (Check Yourself Before You Wreck Yourself)

Remember, you don't have to go whole hog and turn your place into the Sid Vicious of apartment life. You can practice punk shui in your apartment, home, or office in degrees. Some of my clients and friends treat it like a juice fast, only doing it for a week or two, just a limited period of time to jolt them out of their routines. Other clients, myself included, bask in the glow of chaos on a regular basis. Figure out what works for you, and do it. If you just want to tweak one room, or if you want to only do the walls and ceilings, and start bit by bit—that's fine. As long as you are experimenting instead of withdrawing into close-minded oblivion—you're cool.

Baby steps are not all bad. Just as marijuana is called a "gateway" drug, destroying one piece of boring furniture can be your gateway to punk shui.

Displacing Convenience-Induced Patterns

What are convenience-induced patterns? They are habits that don't require you to think, invent, contemplate, or be creative. If we consider the meaning of this definition, it's pretty clear that we have to get rid of these patterns, yes? In fact, you have to change your routine so that you have to think, you have to pay attention, you have to plug in and be engaged with your life, be in the moment and the right-effing-now, wake up, or you'll bang your shin on that gnarly sculpture you put in the doorway of your bedroom. Get it?

Punk shui is not just about a visual aesthetic, it's about changing the space around you so that you wake up, smell the nasty, crappy smells, and the good ones, too, without some prefabricated filter woven by illusion or denial that so many people try to install in their lives. Whatever you use for your illusion-based air freshener, be it a

This is one of my favorite recipes, Cigarette Soup.

plug-in air freshener in your bathroom or cinnamon potpourri, throw that shit out.

This goes for any kind of crappy doily, tablecloth, or flowery curtains. Get rid of anything that is supposed to cover up or beautify, or to numb your senses. Let the light in, look at real surfaces, and embrace the stank-stankity smells and sounds.

Let it go and embrace what comes. Life stinks sometimes—and when it does and you actually deal with it, you become a more respectable, alive, and engaged person.

Displace Shit

Take a moment to think about the fact that you may not even know what the convenient patterns you practice *are* because you're not thinking about them. Take a whole day to notice. Do you drop your keys on a hook by the door? Do you have a coffeemaker that brews coffee automatically in the a.m.? Do you put your feet on an ottoman when you kick back in your La-Z-Boy? Try to stop doing all of these things. See what your life is like without a key hook or an ottoman by your favorite chair. Basically, just make everything harder then it needs to be. You probably do this anyway in most of your life, if you're like your fellow lemmings. At least now it'll be intentional.

For example:

* Where's your alarm clock—by the bed on a nightstand? Too convenient. Put it in another room, turn it up, tune it to the obnoxious station for when it goes off, or even just static. You can also put it under your bed to create maximum tension when it's time to turn it off.

* Put your toothbrush and toothpaste in separate places, far away from your bathroom mirror. Possibly in another room.

* Put your shampoo and soap outside the shower.

* You don't have to keep condiments in the kitchen, or spices on the damn spice rack. Put them in the living room.

* You don't have to have a coffee table in the middle of your living room. Try having a bulky sculpture, a car

tire, or just nothing.

* You don't have to have end tables or a hatrack.
* Don't use your dishwasher for washing dishes.

Punk It Further: Inner Aesthetic

You've got to use your inner aesthetic to design your space around you (an aesthetic not defined by someone else, but by you yourself). When punk shui'ing your place, you need to really consider what you're inner aesthetic is, outside of everyone else's. To get to this point, some people have get rid of a lot of their shit. "We were cuttin' out the filter," Watt says of the days with the Minute Men, when he and D. Boon wrote songs in ways that followed no formula. "They only had to have a beginning, a middle, and an end," and it was okay if they didn't have a bridge. As one of the great punk bands, the Minutemen made their own rules about what was art and what was music. They figured out their inner aesthetic did not need a bridge, as with typical songs. They wanted to play music without that prerequisite. Having written punk operas and hundreds of songs, Watt has broken down barriers in punk music since the early part of his music career as a founding member of the Minutemen. That's what I want you to do—figure out how you want your pad, regardless of the way things are *supposed* to be done. Ignore the rules and do what you want.

Often, as with art and music, the pad can have that same inner aesthetic. Having traveled all over the world and stayed with other artists, Watt says, "Some people's pads are like their art projects, they have energy in them. Can't quantify it. They find art out of life." Some people seem to have an energy in their homes that overrides the details of design. It's not about what to do or how to do it; maybe it's part of being in touch with an inner aesthetic that tells it like it is. The real art comes when the inner aesthetic dictates rather than the outer aesthetic (the outer aesthetic being that which we've learned from others our whole lives and now must dismantle).

Maybe you dig a neat pad where there is order—your definition of order may not connect with anyone else's—whatever. Choose your deal and carry it out, even if it's some type of demented order.

4

Sensory Assault: walls and Ceilings

Walls and ceilings are important elements of punk shui because they surround you, and have the potential to be the biggest and most important elements of your personal design. Making them a part of the home design should be more of a process than just putting up a bunch of weird paintings or painting your whole place black (ah, the cliché).

Walls and ceilings can help a place feel strange

Alexander Eyeballs. (Budman Collection)

or precarious, and will surround you and your guests with whatever atmosphere you're into. Walls are easy to punk out if you learn not to treat them like walls. They are only boundaries in our space if we allow them to be.

White on White

This is a good example of how punk shui'ing apartments can be different for everyone. My punk shui associate TJ decided to go white. I mean white on white on some more white. He made absolutely everything in his apartment stark white. His walls, floors, and ceilings are all painted so white it's blinding.

"I'm going to dye my hair white, too." Even his dog has white hair—seriously.

In this picture, he has painted white canvases and put them on the white walls. He even taped up the windowsills, which were metal, to make them white as well. Now that's *white*.

Some may think clean, white, sterile environs wouldn't fit the chaotic punk shui style, but I see this as a type of sensory deprivation. Either sensory overload or sensory deprivation is extremely punk shui—I like anything that wakes us from the trance of normalcy. TJ made it so that every once in a while there was something in the white apartment that disrupted the white, like a simple black dot. It was as though he was creating a black hole in this seemingly infinite space. I kind of think he did it to get on his own nerves, but I like to think it's one of those black holes from that Roger Rabbit movie, one that you can crawl through and end up in another place.

Sensory Deprivation

One self-awareness guru, Hesh, does sensory deprivation for two hours at a time in one of those tanks. For those who don't know about this, it's a huge, soundproof tank that's completely dark, filled with body-temperature salt water. It's large enough for a person to fit in, but not move around a lot. Originally invented by John C. Lilly, M.D., the tanks were originally used in the 1950s to figure out how workers (like truck drivers or radar observers) with monotonous jobs would cope without interaction or any outside stimulation of the senses. Now they are used by those who enjoy the elaborate states of self-stimulated brain activity they create, and the mind-expanding, peace-induced periods of time when they are left to their own imagination. As Dr. Lilly reported after he did extensive studies in the tank, when you take away the outside world, the brain becomes very active and creative. Hesh's experience in the tank goes like this:

> Your brain needs stimulation, and when you take it away, it creates its own. When I go into the tank and relax, I start to be aware of my heartbeat. Eventually I go into different states of REM, and time stops existing. In one of these sessions I realized that we, as beings, are only breath. At times you just feel electrical energy coursing through your body. When you come out, all of your senses are assaulted and everything experienced is heightened. The sounds are louder and crisper, the light is brighter, and you feel more alive.

This is a great example of what happens when you experiment with your senses. Design in particular is about senses. Punk shui is about shocking them out of their regular, coma-like sleep. It's not a bad idea to see how you can take away the typical things your senses are addicted to and have been brainwashed to depend on (comfortable furniture, the colors you like, crappy TV, and convenience-induced patterns) and see what your mind comes up with in the void. You'll be surprised. Try taking away a few of those "comfort enhancers." That soothing white or pastel on your walls that was there from the college sophomore tenant before you is a comfort enhancer. Get inventive and do some strange things to your walls to stimulate your senses. Walls and ceilings are ideal vehicles to assault our senses.

While designing your pad, start taking into account how color and surroundings affect your senses. Whether it's a tank filled with salt water, a room with white walls and ceilings, or an apartment filled with a bunch of stuff you found in the dump, change the way you see and experience life.

Pay attention to your senses; they're all you've got. Start noticing the way a shocking picture makes you flinch, the way a color all over the ceiling makes you feel trapped or happy. Notice the lighting and the way your brain, eyes, and body respond. Does low light make you feel comfortable and fluorescent light make you feel like a rat in a cage? When you figure out certain relationships, incorporate them into your home.

I had a client, Marcia, who took all of the light coverings off the lamps and overhead lights in one room. She painted one wall fuchsia, another booger green, the third bright orange, and put mirrors on the fourth. She put a dead plant in the corner and burned some nasty incense so that the whole place just reeked. In the next room she put low lights, comfortable furniture, light gray walls that were pleasant to look at, and usually played nice low music. She saved the good incense for this room. She loved the shock caused by going from one room to another. "It's like jumping into cold water on a hot summer's day. A complete shocker. It keeps me awake. I like taking guests to the bright, abrasive room first, and then to the gray room. It makes them love the gray room even more—although some like it freaky, too."

Another couple of clients have a totally normal two-bedroom house, with completely traditional décor. But they left one bedroom unfinished, replete with sheetrock and bare floors. The walls are unpainted, and it's furnished with folding chairs and an army cot. Whenever they get sick of their Pottery Barn bedroom, they spend the night in the other bedroom for a break.

It's not just about loud colors, garish lighting, and bad smells. Take it further. Weird art provokes some strange emotions—it can be a picture of a naked woman, or of a grotesquely mutilated farm animal. A blank wall gives you a good opportunity to choose images and art that make you or others uncomfortable. We could go on all day about the artists who have used these methods of shocking art; this is one tradition I don't mind continuing. I believe that provoking thoughts and feelings is a great way to stimulate energy in a room.

Here are two pictures I did. One of them depicts an invisible man hanging himself as his black wingtips fall forward off a broken ladder, giving your imagination something to feast on. It sits opposite a bloody soiled pillow that's been nailed to the wall. The pillow is absolutely disgusting, and when people see it, they say, "What the fuck is that? Why is that pillow bleeding?" I like that.

My client Jill dated this guy named Bob for a while. Everyone thought he was a complete slob, but he swore that he knew where everything was. His apartment would give you headaches if you looked at it long enough. He was an industrial sculptor and had scraps of metal lying everywhere, old pieces of rock, wood, and machines on his desk and sofa, and a lot of crap on the floor.

The thing that I remember the most was the way he posted all of his ideas on the wall. Any time he did a drawing about anything or had

an idea for a sculpture, he tacked it on the wall. There were hundreds
of sheets of paper littering the wall, with all of these really fascinating
(and sometimes not) things drawn on them. You could stand there for
hours looking at them. Okay, so that's how it is for a visitor. Imagine
how it was for him: any creative idea you've ever had is staring you in

the face all the time, basically saying something like, "Don't forget that you wanted to make a piece of furniture out of the old airplane rudder in your closet." His walls were constantly overwhelming his senses. I would guess that sometimes he found it inspiring and other times maddening, because most of us like to forget about ideas we've never fulfilled.

Precarious Hangings

Your senses are going to be heightened in a big way if you feel that you're constantly in danger of something falling on you. Check out the following examples.

It's a pretty common thing in small apartments: most people hang their bikes in their apartments against the wall. I decided to put mine in the doorway between the living room and the bedroom so I have to do a little limbo dance on the way through the door.

This is a mobile that my friend Si's grandfather made. It's made of jagged-edged copper pieces. Mobiles are a good way to hang art from your ceiling. The sharper and heavier, the better. Hang art at

weird angles and secure it so it looks like it's going to fall off the wall and onto your guests.

Don't Fix Light Fixtures

This is an expensive chandelier that was broken. It casts really interesting shadows on the ceiling and walls. It also has sharp, jagged edges that are a little gnarly—and it's nice and simple.

Bashing light fixtures with a baseball bat is a great way to alter the lighting and lend a different mood to the room—and let's face it, nothing says punk shui better than a bunch of shattered lightbulbs and lamps.

On your walls, you can also make your own light-switch covers. This is a good way to get an unfinished look (but thankfully not in a way that Rachel Ashwell had in mind).

Weird light fixtures can cast a strange glow on a room. No fixture is good. Bare bulbs can transform a room.

My friend Stephen had an apartment with no electricity, and he used flashlights for everything. This is one way to go. No electricity presents some very interesting possibilities—it casts everything in a different light, if you will.

Lighting everything with candles is a good idea, too. I've been

54   Punk Shui

through two New York City blackouts. One of them was everything below 14th Street and the other was everything east of Ohio. During the one below 14th Street, I was working at a bar, the Fat Black Pussy-cat, and we closed the doors, only admitted locals, burned candles, and had free drinks. The coolest things about candles, if you choose to use them in your place, is that they create lively and moving shadows,

which, of course, gives your joint a different "energy."

Wall Dressings

Blood on the wall: this is a guaranteed way to make a strong first impression. Nothing says "yikes" like smears of blood-red across a stark white wall. Apply it as you would paint or stain. You can order pork blood from your local butcher, or have it shipped to you via an online service such as www.hemostat.com. It's perfectly safe—just don't drink it. Good times!

I had one client, Tim, who lined his friends up against the wall and shot them with a paint gun to leave their outlines all over the wall. He says, "I don't have many friends any more, but they've all left their marks on my walls and floors."

Holes: While you don't have to punch a hole in your wall to participate in punk shui, if you're not opposed to it (or attached to the deposit you gave your landlord), it's a remarkably cathartic exercise. Instruments like baseball bats, or even a piece of furniture, are okay for weak walls, but usually a goodold-fashioned sledgehammer is the way to go. Don't use your hand if you're pissed, we've all seen that scenario played out in the movies—you'll hurt your hand, dude.

Peeling paint or wallpaper can make a place feel dilapidated in a good way. You can use a variety of tools, including razors and sandpaper, to distress your walls. The older the wall treatment or paint job, the better.

Anything on the Wall

Find objects that don't belong on the wall and attach them to the wall. This is an old Martin Backpacker guitar that I found smashed up. Before I hung it on the wall, it was a broken and useless guitar. And now it's art.

This fan is a good example of nontraditional things that work well on the wall. Anything that is "mountable" is good. Putting the fan on the wall was extremely functional because it moved the air around the room much better this way that it did on the desk. By experimenting with this, I found a functional solution to a problem when I least expected it.

Putting all types of 3D on walls can be interesting.

Put together your own mural, whether by painting or gluing

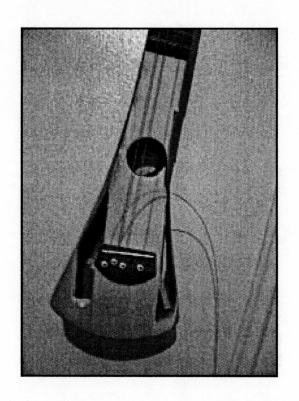

pieces of glass, mirror, fabric, or wood to your wall in any design (or indiscernible nondesign). Put pictures where you wouldn't expect them. By putting a picture on the front of a shelf, you have to reach around it to get something on the interior of the shelf. It makes it into a cabinet and gives it a different look.

(Courtesy Norman Gosney.)

Do a Pollock—get some paints and go crazy. Even if you've never painted in your life, act like you are an artist. Even if you're not—there is no wrong way to do it. (As you know by now, substance use is not discouraged.) By using the walls as your palettes, and putting huge amounts of paint on them, you can come up with some really nice thick textured surfaces. Incorporating other things into the paint can lead to different levels of texture—I've used everything from Cocoa Puffs to nails (I tacked them on separately to make sure they'd stick). Whatever is immediately on hand can help you make your decision.

My associate Gage made an incredible piece of art that involves neon lights over photographs. Take a hint from your trailer-trash relatives, and use outdoor siding, aluminum or vinyl (without question the most heinous design substance ever created), for indoor wall dressing.

Ceilings

Don't forget your ceiling. Most people ignore them, but a shockingly orange ceiling can really change a room. For one of my clients, Jose, I found an old ceiling fan that wobbles when it turns. It's a beautiful piece that complements his whole living room. The wobble on this fan is six inches to a foot. It's perfectly safe, I think, but it really freaks people out with its crazy-sounding creaking noise. The noise constantly implies the piece will be airborne at any time.

A punk shui original favorite is a stalactite-stucco ceiling with different lengths of pointed sculptures and pieces hanging down. These ceilings always remind me of a dramatic version of when Nicolas Cage scrapes his knuckles on the stucco ceiling during his fight with John Goodman in *Raising Arizona*. You can use plaster to make the spikes.

Windows

Sometimes light is good and sometimes it's just plain bad. Manipulate your moods using your windows. Major ch'i comes from windows, and you can create a really interesting atmosphere if you allow yourself to experiment.

By blocking your windows with weird objects, like paintings, sculptures, dummies, or mannequins, you can alter appearances inside and out. As a wise man once said, "You can only see light from darkness."

Use window dressings in different ways. Break them, hang them upside down. Check out the creative use of these shades.

Painting on windows can create bizarre light in a room. When the light filters through the windows, it also does interesting things to the paint itself. One of my clients, Chris, tried blocking the light. By using old sheets and weird posters and paintings, he completely blocked the light from his bedroom. He actually found that it was far from uncomfortable at times, and that he really enjoyed the darkness of his

bedroom in the morning: "I don't like getting up in the morning at all, so I don't like the sun coming in my windows, waking me up. I'm also in the middle of the woods, so I always feel that when I don't have sheets on the windows, things are looking in. When I leave my house, I'm almost blinded by the sunlight. It's like I'm entering a different

world. I basically use the sheets in particular because they're the clos-
est and easiest things to tack up on the walls and windows." As mentioned previously, you don't have to spend a lot of money to mess
with your traditional, boring ways of decorating.

Berman's pad.

5

Live in the Room

The Living Room

I'm not saying that you can't watch TV—but let's be real here. We have proof that it is an extreme waste of time. In fact, in the ol' punk shui lab, we did a very scientific study. We took ten people from completely different backgrounds and asked them to watch about thirty hours of TV a week for a month. We found that for each hour spent watching TV, nine out of ten subjects were about ten times lamer and less creative than before. The documented, specific differences we found were that they were more boring to talk to, they had less of a sense of humor, and they had much lamer digs. And—this was the thing that really turned my stomach—they had almost no sex drive. Jesus.

For the sake of preserving your sexuality and all-important character development, try to do something constructive or destructive with your time rather than watch crappy TV. Therefore, when designing your home, even if you don't blow up your TV, you should make it a very minor part of your living room. As you can see—not everyone watches TV:

"I don't watch TV." —Mike Watt

"I don't watch TV." —Norman Gosney

"I don't watch TV." —Jesus

"I only watch TV when I masturbate." —Josh Hughes

Dumpster Diving Is an Art

Instead of watching TV, try looking for entertainment by venturing into garbage receptacles for old possessions and all things thrown

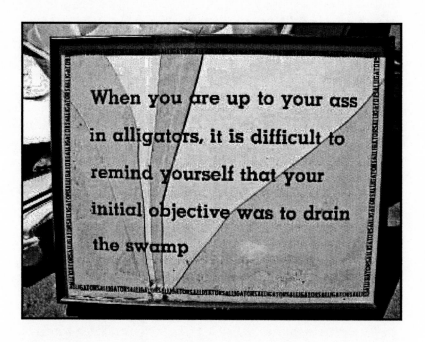

When you are up to your ass in alligators, it is difficult to remind yourself that your initial objective was to drain the swamp

away. Really. You'd be surprised at how alive you feel when you dive deep into a Dumpster nearby, break into someone's home to steal the sofa of your dreams, or even just try to lug a fifty-pound piece of furniture down the street. Adrenaline rush, here you come.

Seriously, furniture or art found on the street is a great way to decorate your pad on the cheap. Dumpster diving doesn't have to be exclusive to Dumpsters. It can also include really great things that people have left on the street or in their yards for the garbage truck. It can include secondhand stores. Basically, the only criterion is that the object be ready for its second or third life, and not brand-new. Maybe someone rejected it, maybe they beat it, maybe they loved it and moved on, maybe their girlfriend threw it out because she was redecorating their apartment after trashing the bachelor pad. Who knows, but for whatever reason, people throw away good stuff.

To go Dumpster diving, you have to do a couple of very minor mindset alterations:

> 1. Remove yourself from the brain-sucking ideas that retailers have been banging into your head, dictating that you have to have something new, with a price tag, added to your pad on a regular basis. Liberate yourself, become an anarchist where consumption is concerned, and know that purchase size doesn't equal penis size. And for you women out there (I remain true to my own definition of "gentleman" by letting you fill in the blank), purchase

doesn't equal————size. (I guess that doesn't exactly work as well, but you know what I mean.)

2. Open your mind to the universe, and know that if you do this, and if you have no standards or preconceptions

about what you want, and if you give no credit to trends or superficial glossy looks, you will end up with something much cooler and more interesting that will work for your place in ways you can't imagine.

3. Allow yourself to be unconditional about when and how you "go" Dumpster diving. Develop an accepting mindset that allows universal energy (good or bad) to flow to you through objects that appear directly in or outside your path. You will find things at any given time in the oddest, strangest situations. You might see something on your way to work or on your way home from a bar at four in the morning, or you might intentionally go and find something because you're sick of looking at your own shit. Either way, consider lugging that nasty-ass chair home (even when it's eaten through by rats and roaches) because you need a chair, or maybe you like the woodcarving on the back of it. Something strikes you about it, even though you know others might cringe at the oddball look that was probably conceived by

some furniture designer in the haze of the vinyl-pleather love-fest of the sixties. For some reason, it suddenly may feel like it was meant to be. What the hell, if you get it home and find out it sucks, you'll toss it back onto the street.

Acceptance of these poor little orphaned relics of another decade and another set of aesthetics altogether different is what punk shui is about. Perhaps we have no choice, because, as fate would have

it, it was placed in our path, left in our apartment by a former tenant, or even given to us as a present from a roommate who was too lame to move everything they didn't want. Or maybe we make the choice and take the little crappy piece of design home from its lonely perch on the street and put it in our pad and, believe it or not, it looks kind of cool.

A Few Tips for Dumpster-Diving Trips

My client Rob Lanham tells us about what Dumpster diving did for his living room:

> Even if I made lots of money and could afford "nice" furniture, I would still try to find street finds . . . I find most of my furniture on the street. In fact, the other day I had a friend come over and he asked me where I got this green chair I had found on the street. He said, "I just threw that out two weeks ago." I said, "Why? It's a great chair!" and he said, "I know, I just didn't have room for it."

When asked if he had any tips for other Dumpster divers, Rob said one of the best things to do is to watch the calendar. "On the first and the end of each month is when people move, and when they put their trash and furniture on the curb." That's an excellent strategy. If you're going to be organized (which, I have to say, can be construed as somewhat nerdy and un-punk), that's the way to do it.

You can actually decorate your whole place with other people's throwaways. Maura Jasper, coauthor of *Punk Rock Aerobics,* said of using found objects, "I love my apartment, it's full of all kinds of fun stuff from yard sales and trash picking. It inspires me to know that a person can live so nicely from others peoples waste."

Other People's Throwaway Erotic Oeuvre

My associate Brian Ermanski, a painter, had a unique experience during one of his routine dives into a trash bin. When he dove into this particular Dumpster, he dug deep to the bottom and found bags of artwork by a man he later discovered was named Edward P. Victus. Afterwards, Brian found out that Mr. Victus had become sick with pneumonia and had to have a nurse. "All his porn drawings and cutouts of nudes were all over the furniture and the walls of his whole apartment, and his toilet and the bathroom—his whole apartment was covered with porn. Not to disturb the nurse, his family agreed to throw it all out," Brian said.

When he found the bags of art, Brian dragged them out on Lafayette Street and began displaying them and asking for donations. "I was astonished that his friends would throw this stuff out," Brian later told the New York Times, which ran an article titled "Artist's Erotic Oeuvre Is Rescued from the Trash."*

Brian had a few tips for Dumpster-diving enthusiasts:

* ✱ "Don't judge a book by its cover...you have to dig deep to find something good. The majority of good stuff is gone because it's on the top."

* ✱ "If there are bags, check inside, because I didn't see any artwork until I opened up a bag, and when I did, there

*New York Times, February 10, 2005.

were like five hundred paintings in this one garbage bag."

As per Brian's experience, you never know what furniture or art you'll find for the main room in your pad.

Dumpster Diving in Junk Stores

And of course, there is the Dumpster diving of the shopping world; junk stores, Salvation Army, Goodwill, garage sales, and estate sales are great places to find furniture to work with. Usually, the more out of the way, the better. There's this place called Hohenwald, Tennessee, population around four thousand. I'm from Tennessee, so I used to go there sometimes. Mainly, I went there to shop at what the locals called "junk stores." These stores are fantastic, because they haven't been discovered and abused by the droves of hipster people who swarm any junk stores or Goodwills in metropolitan areas and ruin them for well-meaning punk shui enthusiasts. These hipsters and artists usually take all the good stuff from good, old-fashioned junk stores, or turn them into places like "Cheap Jacks" in Manhattan, where a pair of secondhand jeans costs about ten percent less than it would at a snobby boutique in Soho. Anyway, these junk stores are great because everything is CHEAP (our veritable middle name) and authentically secondhand.

Another really phenomenal thing about junk stores, at least in Hohenwall, is that they operate in massive amounts of junk. The large ones actually have some type of indoor crane, which releases a giant pile of newly arrived clothes onto a huge warehouse floor for eager customers to peruse. Actually, it requires a different kind of perusing than typical shopping. You have to use your whole body, squatting on the floor to tunnel deep through favorites like Duck Head, Polo and Levi's, or adventure through stacks of furniture. Most of the clothes and furniture are really damn cheap. These are the places that "vintage" store owners travel to when they want to find clothes, like a shirt for two dollars, and mark it up to fifty dollars in their store in Los Angeles.

Outfitting your living room and other rooms in the house with used furniture (and clothes for that matter) is a good way to begin punking it out. Sometimes all it takes is a good, solid piece to set the mood.

Altering/Slashing Furniture

You can see clearly that one of the first things I did to my living room to spice it up was to saw the sofa in half. Sawing apart any piece of furniture is not for the faint of heart, but it certainly lends a different feel to your living room. As I've said before, if you can't figure out where to start, begin by working on a part of your living room, or a piece of furniture that has been pissing you off. In my case, I had a red couch that I always thought was a little too, ah, how do you say... *available* to anyone who wanted to crash at my apartment. It always seemed to be a magnet for visitors who, upon planting their asses in the couch, decided it was so comfortable they wanted to spend the night. Anyway, when I took a look around my living room, that was the piece I decided to attack right away. The couch is totally different now. It definitely adds something to the apartment, and I don't have quite as many vagrants crashing because it's a little harder

to stretch across it now.

Altering furniture is a great way to completely change the mood of the living room. And as you know, the living space can be a really intrinsic part of a home. This is probably one of the most dramatic ways to punk shui your home. There aren't any 1-2-3 steps that make this an easily quantifiable procedure, but I'll give you some tips:

★ Use whatever you have nearby for doing this. If you have to use one piece of furniture to bash another—you kill two birds with one stone.

★ Refer to the section "Implements of Destruction" in chapter 3. Axes, baseball bats, guns, screwdrivers, and sledgehammers are quite useful.

★ Remember, whatever use the furniture was put to in its previous life, it doesn't have to serve the same purpose now. A chair can become a hanging on the wall after the legs are bashed in. A coffee table's leg can now be used to prop a door open after it has been elegantly sculpted into a splintered wedge.

★ You can have a party with friends as you reinvent the way your furniture can be used (we'll cover parties in chapter 9). Sometimes getting creative requires more than one perspective.

Remaking Furniture

This is a picture of a chair that was falling apart, which we made into a table that looked like a chair. Why? Well, first off, we never said punk shui made sense—in fact, the less sense it makes, the better. This chair in particular definitely prompts a second glance from most, and it implies that things may not be what they appear.

This is a picture of a broken cabinet that holds broken glass. A lot of people feel shitty after they break a wine glass, a plate, or a mirror (especially if they have good solid Catholic guilt). This cabinet is perfect for putting those mistakenly or intentionally broken pieces on display. You don't have to worry about disposing of the jagged edges, either, and you now have a semifunctional sculpture that also can be used as a receptacle.

This is a really nice piece. My clients Stephen and Kyle have this in their loft in Nashville. The bottom part is a tanning bed, and it's been converted to a couch. Not only does it give this fatally retarded contraption another life, but it also creates a nice deco look.

As per the tools that we discussed earlier in the book, this is a

piece where the gun was used for reworking this chair. It's great to sit in, was fun to shoot at, and looks amazing. If I use it to sit on the street, when it rains, the water drains through—pretty handy. This chair was

86 Punk Shui

also the subject of a video piece that is currently on my website. On the video, you can see me shoot the hell out of the chair.

Bill, owner of Ocean Surf Shop, told us how he has been remaking old lamps by mixing up parts and pieces. "I've been doing these lamps that you get out of the trash, taking part A lamp and then put-

88　Punk Shui

ting it in part B of another lamp...making it into a different lamp."
Mixing the different components of one piece of furniture or lamp
can create interesting hybrids of style and era.

Turning Japanese

Be aware of the style of furniture you've always taken for granted. Try
to make your concept of what furniture is a lot broader—for example, think about the kind of furniture we have here in America opposed to other cultures and how it affects us.

Brad Warner, author of *Hardcore Zen: Punk Rock, Monster Movies,
& the Truth About Reality,* just moved back to the States after living in
Tokyo for more than a decade. Originally a punk rock musician, he
now writes and works for a monster movie company. His dwellings in
Tokyo helped him get out of his Western mindset. His pad in Japan
was authentically Japanese. He had almost no furniture; it was replaced by tatami mats and a Japanese-style table around a foot tall for
the middle of the room. He sat on the floor all the time. Since recently moving to L.A., he lives in an American-style furnished apart-

ment his company found for him. "I have a couch, but I sit on the floor because I can't deal with sitting on the couch because . . . when you sit on a Western-style couch you're forced into bad posture. On this typical American big fluffy couch there's no way you can sit up straight. You're slumped over . . . and I immediately fall asleep." By using different cultural practices, you can get a more objective view of the unconscious acceptance you've had all of your life about living habits, space, and how you use your furniture. Completely changing the way you regard chairs and sofas can change the way you think about a room.

Rooting out all those things you've always taken for granted will alter the way you wake up in the morning, go to sleep, and live in your abode. One of the things I suggest to my clients is sitting on the floor for a week, rather than using chairs and sofas, to get a different perspective. Maybe, by the end of it, you'll be totally fine with trashing and destroying your chairs, and then you can put them on the wall.

Furniture Placement

Sometimes, if my clients aren't into destroying everything (or even if they are), I focus on placing furniture creatively in the living room, in some way that renders it semifunctional and possibly, in its unique way, aesthetically pleasing. Besides the aesthetic assault one experiences with a punk shui piece, there should also be an assault on the way we typically assume social interactions will work in a room. The living room is a great place to change the dynamics through furniture placement.

Remember, the living room is where you live. Period. *How* you live is up to you. Design, art, and positioning determine the quality of your life, and the way you embrace that energy. By turning chairs toward the wall, putting a mirror on the floor, or putting sharp objects that one must step over in commonly used pathways in the living room and halls—you're heightening your own consciousness and doing the same for anyone who visits.

One of my clients, Cindy, put her mirror on her hallway floor and a wood sculpture of a little man in the middle of her living room. On the way to the living room, she and her guests had to step over the mirror. The sculpture was about four feet high. People sitting in the living room had to maneuver around the sculpture when they wanted to talk to someone on the other side of it. It created some pretty fraught conversations.

Look around your living room. Do you have end tables, a coffee table, and furniture placed in a socially convenient way? Have you ever really thought about why you do that? If people really want to speak to each other, they shouldn't need you to give them a hand-job for providing the privilege. I mean, you're already supplying the room. Let people make their own way in the world. It's every man for herself. Get creative about how you arrange the living room. Rethink everything—make no assumptions. Do people even need to sit? What is the first thing they notice when they come into the room? Maybe it should be that it doesn't feel like any living room they have ever entered—in fact, maybe it doesn't even feel like a living room.

I had a client, Ralph, who wanted to really shake up the living room arrangement, and I put his bookshelf against the door so that the thing could only open a quarter of the way. We also arranged his couch so that it faced the wall, attached his coffee table to the wall, put the recliner on its side so that you couldn't really sit on it (the cushions went on the floor instead).

Ralph also got creative, scraped his lame Twisted Sister and red Lamborghini posters off the wall, and did some of his own art with broken bottles and cans, and put them on the wall instead. I think it looks pretty stupid now, but you should have seen it before.

Constantly Shifting

"Some people think they should do up their place and then live with it for a long time. I can't think of anything worse." Jim Budman, owner of Budman's Studio and a great friend, gives this advice to those new to punk shui:

"Create a little bit of disorder. It is really important to move things around, and that's . . . what punk shui is about. So many people think they have to decorate or design a space and they have to live with it for five years, ten years until they get tired of it and are going to redo it. To me that is so foolish, to me it is so important to move things around and create not only your own order but a little bit of your disorder. That's what punk shui does. Move art, don't be afraid to move it from one room to another, and all of a sudden it will take on a whole new life. You change pieces of furniture . . . it makes your living and working situation all that much more interesting and exciting. When you entertain and people come over, they notice the change and it's new and different, and you can do it without spending one dime!"

6

in the Bedroom

Think about what we call this room. The living room makes okay sense, to a degree. There is a lot of room to interpret. It's a room we live in. When we take a close look at the word *bedroom,* does that tell us it is supposed to be a room in which we only have a bed? What about living? What about sleeping? And, hey, here's the most important question—what about sex? Names give things power. They force us into unconscious assumptions that can make us assume what to do with that space, what to put into it and what to do when we're in there. A lot of people, probably the same people who think they have to center a living room around a TV, think the bedroom is merely the room in which they put a bed and sleep. How limited can you get? Think of other names for the bedroom. You can just call it "my room." Whatever floats your boat—just try to get away from the norm.

A Room Without a Bed

Your "bedroom" doesn't have to have a bed. You can sleep in your living room—who said you even had to have a bedroom? Rethink the whole concept and get creative. I can guarantee that if you start sleeping in your kitchen, you will have a new perspective on life.

My client Casey used to love to sleep in his bathtub, but that's probably because he had a little drinking problem. He told me, "It was great because I could puke all over myself and never had to change the sheets." Of course, he was single.

Dracula had it down—he slept in a coffin, and if that's not punk shui, I don't know what is. I actually built a coffin for one of my clients who was pretty goth. His name was Doom. He even slept with the lid on. Talk about freaking out some dates.

Try sleeping on your couch, on your living room floor, or in the bathroom. It's not a bad idea to check out your life without that big, padded mattress you've grown accustomed to that keeps you from feeling the bumps, the cold floor, and the less enchanting dreams.

The Place Where You Lay Your Head

If you're really attached to the concept of beds, at least go your own way and be original. No futons, because that's hack punk shui.

One of my clients and I found a king-size waterbed from the eighties for her little studio in the East Village. It was hell getting the thing up the stairs; we had to take it apart. If you've ever slept in one of those, you know—if anyone is with you and lies down while you're on the bed, it jostles you, or, worst-case scenario, rockets you out of the bed. This can definitely liven up the typical bedroom experience.

If you want to get fancy, take a full-size piece of thick plywood and put it on four cinder blocks. I do this for some clients who get trapped in the whole headboard/footboard thing that typical stores are pushing.

The bedroom is where you start your day, so it's important not to be too comfortable, because you want to get up and get to the world. That's why, for a few of my clients, I came up with some interesting ways to keep them on their toes while they snoozed. I found these really terrific army bunk beds for one of my clients, and turned the bottom one into a couch and left the top one for him to sleep in. The biggest adjustment he faced was rolling out of the bed in his sleep and falling five feet to the floor—ouch!

For those claustrophobics out there, if you have an issue of space, I came up with a great way to incorporate this phobia into your bedroom. One of my clients decided to build a bed with plywood, but instead of putting it on cinder blocks, she put it on two-by-fours and positioned the mattress so that it was very high, about a foot from the ceiling. She told me, "I learned very quickly not to sit up in bed when I heard a strange sound in the house—I have a few bumps on my forehead to prove it. At first it was a real-life nightmare. But I did get a great closet out of the underside of my bed. I put doors on it and hung all my clothes in there."

Another client kept his original bed, but we experimented with the sheets. They say morning is the best time for creativity, so, to take advantage of that, we got some sheets made out of paper and he kept a pen by the bed to write down his dreams or thoughts—he just had to watch out for paper cuts.

If you have issues with space, meaning lack thereof, one option is to use a Japanese futon (not like the American futon), because they take up almost no space when not in use. They are thin mats that can be rolled up and put in the closet after you wake up. Think of all the space that that opens up in a room, when you don't have a giant, American-style bed taking up your bedroom—especially you New Yorkers with studios. Here are a few subtle ways to punk out your traditional bedroom:

* Put your bed under a window so you can hear street sounds. A little shrieking from a bum or a siren can serve as a lullaby. The bed also serves as an obstacle when opening and closing the window.

* Use the bed as obstacle for everything. Put it against

the door to obstruct the entrance to your room.

★ Toss the bedside table—who needs a sip of water within arm's reach, or an alarm clock blaring. Instead, use it as a guinea pig for that new tool you just got.

★ Practice sleeping with the lights on—your ability to do this proves you might be a true punk shui master.

Overall, just try to realize that our accepted ways of organizing are just what people told us to do. As to your own design, that is up for definition. There is no right or wrong way to do anything.

Fuck Shui

Now that we've gone over different options for sleeping and beds, let's get to the important stuff. Consider the things you do or don't do in the bedroom. I hope you're having sexual intercourse somewhere, or you're at least trying to have sexual intercourse, or alternately you're thinking about having sexual intercourse while you make love to yourself in the morning. Regardless, know this to be true—if you have a boring bedroom design, you'll probably have a boring sex life.

Allowing yourself to dwell in a typical bedroom (predictable arrangement of dresser drawers, bed and bookshelf) is only furthering your tendency to get into an intimacy habit (by the way, in this scenario, habits suck!). We all know what this is, right? This is quite possibly one of the most depressing things you can begin to do with another person. Same person, same drug(s), same restaurant, same foreplay, same bed, same smells, same lighting, same forced cries of delight, same position, same time (if you actually go thirty minutes, you feel like a champ), same required holding time afterwards, and, of course, if you're a smoker... well, you get it. This, my friends, is what a typical bedroom setup can lead to! For some of my more lonely clients, years and years of this makes bad porn feel like the best sex they've ever had. I've had clients come to me in this condition. It's a condition they don't often talk about, and they may not even tell their best friends. No lust, no love, no living, no getting off and no getting it on. Now, *that* is the ultimate complacency. That is the kind of complacency which you have to fight, tooth and nail, until your last breath. By getting creative in the bedroom, you can turn your sex life around.

Here are some tips that are proven to open up your bedroom to the positive elements of "fuck shui." (The term, by the way, was coined by my punk shui associate Norman Gosney.)

* Your bed should be moved. If the head of it is against a wall or corner, and feels "safe," then you should try to make it so that you can't see the door when you're lying down. This adds to the feeling of danger and abandon, since you never know what or who might come through it. As everybody knows, the thrill of being caught is like one of the top three non-food-based aphrodisiacs or something.

* Instead of just thinking creative sex is about trying a new position—try a new position in a new location besides the bed. Avoid having sex on the bed, because the next thing you'll know it's missionary time, and then you're asleep.

* Personally, I love sleeping on the beach, and it's great for sex. So why not put a sandbox in your room for a bed. Get a bunch of shells and a cheesy tape of waves

crashing and go to work. Just watch out for the crabs.

For those of you going through a period of abstinence, you might as well re-create prison life and ditch the bed frame and headboard. Put your mattress on the floor, sans sheets.

Your Threads

Often, people store their clothes in the bedroom. There are several options for how and where to store clothes. I don't usually keep all of my clothes in anything in particular—no dresser, closet, or hangers. I keep them in stacks around my bedroom and sometimes in my kitchen. But I do keep some things in a dresser, which I lay on the floor.

Any piece of furniture can be laid on its side or on its back instead of upright, and it lends a whole different feel to a room. With my dresser on the floor, all I have to do is lift the drawer—it works out fine. It also gives me more space on my walls to play around with. It's a good idea to use clothes as décor around the apartment. Lingerie nailed to the wall of any room definitely sets the tone. I have a

client, Nat, who does that. "I get immediate reactions from my dates. Then I know which way they swing, how kinky they are, or if I gross them out. It's a good thing to know before you start a relationship." Another client, Marcus, tried the clothes-all-over-the-apartment technique and said, "I know it seems like a pain in the ass, but they're al-

ways right there and I never have to fold them. And it makes the floor soft."

This really works well if you want to break in your clothes and you'd like them to have a worn-out, tattered look.

Worship the Clutter

You're probably sick of feeling that you need to clean out that damn closet because things fall on your head every time you open the door to look for something. You may have stuff in the corners of your place that you know you should have thrown away a long time ago. You might even feel guilty that you kept old shoes, broken musical instruments, crappy lamps, or old electrical appliances, but you can't seem to get rid of them because you think you may at some point (a) use them, (b) fix them, or (c) give them to someone who really needs them. Or, (d) you're just a lazy asshole.

Whatever the case, you can change the way you deal with clutter. Let's put it this way: clutter is like quicksand; if you fight it, it only pulls you into the muck deeper. If you worship it, and by this we mean get creative with it, you can really change the way your place feels, and you can do it inexpensively.

How to Worship Clutter

I had a bike that was half broken, and I refused to throw it away. The bike had had both of the wheels stolen off it, and all that was left was a bike seat. Finally, I got my tools out and made a stool out of the seat.

The seat illustrates the fundamental principles of punk shui. When you sit on it, you really have to be aware to sit on it and focus, or you'll fall off. It's not comfortable at all. Maybe you've seen those designer seats resembling inflatable beach balls without back or arm support, which people are using in their offices and homes. The same idea applies with my chair—you have to focus and use other parts of your body besides your lazy ass. I use it when I type, and it makes me focus on my work to get it done quickly, so I can move to the couch for a much-deserved nap. Use clutter, and use it well. Don't worry about it messing up your apartment. Make it into something better. Make it work for you. A lot of people say they like sparse open space with as little clutter as possible, but I think clutter can be functional. Clutter utilizes space. It may not be efficient, but that's a word that's not in my vocabulary and is way too familiar to those in, dare I say, corporate environments.

I'll make a generalization: people who have a bunch of crap in their possession are usually much cooler. An old boss of mine, Tom, had an entire airplane hangar filled with stuff that he had collected and stored over the years. He sent me in there one day to look for something, and I found a jeep. It ran and everything. I told him and he had completely forgotten about it. It was as if he had a new car. That just shows you being a packrat can pay off. Try to incorporate clutter with not only your bedroom, but all of your rooms.

Clutter can become art in many senses. And that brings me to

Mike Watt's house.

my next piece of punk shui advice—put some art in your bedroom. I know that people typically think a more public room is where they have a good bit of art, but I think it really helps your creative juices flow when you go to sleep and wake up surrounded by inspiring pieces of art.

Punk It Further: What Are Rooms?

I've been giving you the skinny on what I do with my client's rooms. Particular punk shui methods for particular rooms work for a lot of my clients, who have certain levels of punk shui they're ready for. Making punk shui methods unique to each room is not the only way to go. In fact, it is only part of the way. It is only half the battle. The very fact that we believe we are limited to rooms and define them by their traditional uses is absurd, if you consider it. I mean, why do we only have to denote one room for "beds," another for "living," and another for an office? Isn't our non-inquisitive habit of following in these traditional arrangements a little strange? Have you ever considered your living space without these confines?

Go the extra mile and dare yourself to find out what happens when you break down the boundaries, the walls and the normal arrangements of homes. What if you had no designated purpose for any of the rooms in your house? If you take this approach, you begin to break down other creative boundaries that have prevented you from living to your fullest, least BS-hindered potential. As we go on to talk about how to punk out your kitchen and bathrooms—think for a moment. How would you arrange your home if you didn't have the predisposition, from years of programming, to just have the typical divisions that make up living rooms, bedrooms, offices, dens, kitchens, and bathrooms?

7

kitschy kitchens

The Kaotic Kitchen

The kitchen is often one of the more organized rooms in a home. You know, everything in its place and all of that. But now it's time to embrace displacement. Nothing should go where it's supposed to in the punk shui kitchen. Put the dish drainer on the floor; put your pans in a stack on the counter. Forget convenience; like Lindsay Lohan's breasts, organization is merely an illusion.

My Kitchen

I personally like my kitchen a little off-kilter. For example, everything about my table is precarious. If you want this effect with your IKEA kitchen table, twist the legs off your table, go outside and beat the dog with them—just kidding, you can beat them on the fire escape. Mine

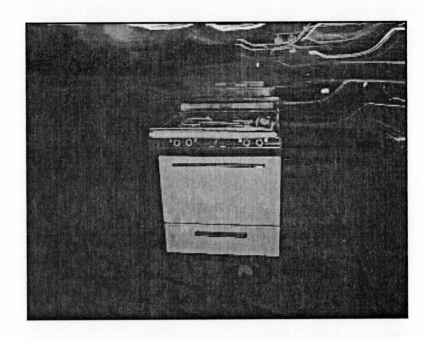

were aluminum legs—they were really loud. My landlord actually freaked out and came up because he thought someone had been shot.

The dishes that I own do not match, whatsoever, and are cracked in places. Broken dishes are helpful in the punk shui'ed kitchen; not

only do they reek of domesticity gone wrong, but they can be hung from the ceiling, arranged on the wall as a poor imitation of one of those creepy dish collections, or smashed on the floor for a bed of ceramic shards (make sure you wear shoes when walking on this one). I once made a mural out of broken dishes on the wall of one of my clients' kitchens. As I've said before, don't throw anything away; rather take things that have been thrown away and display them in all their discarded, empty glory.

In my kitchen, everything can be really messed up because I don't use it often. I mostly live on take-out. That's why I can get pretty freaky with my kitchen. Recently I used a couple of old toilets as seats for my messed-up kitchen table. Sometimes I also use the toilet bowls for chips at parties. Anything goes, and believe me, if people get hungry enough or are riddled with the munchies—the chip receptacle doesn't matter.

How to Make a Punk Shui Oven

When I actually do cook, I don't use an oven or a microwave. The new instrument for cooking is this contraption:

It's called the punk shui oven. Basically it's a piece of wood with two nails jutting out. You take a cord from a lamp or a radio and splice the wire. You then wrap the wire around each nail. If you plug the cord in and you stick a hot dog on the nail, it will cook the hot dog in a few seconds.

Attention, dumb fucks: DO NOT ACTUALLY MAKE ONE OF THESE.

Issues with Food

Sometimes with clients, I try to get them to embrace or confront their favorite or least favorite things about food in the kitchen. One client, Steve, is a huge meat lover. He has pieces of cured ham and

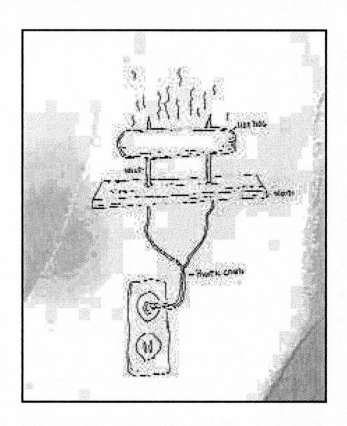

pork, some even a foot long, hanging from his ceiling. "I love meat hanging around me when I cook, and if I need any, I just cut if right off." Another client, Yolanda, has some serious body image problems because she's been reading way too many glossy magazines (which we burned in her sink to celebrate her punk shui efforts).

She now has all sorts of pictures of her in her bathing suit posted around her kitchen. She even has one blown up, so it's life-size. Needless to say, she eats only healthy fruits and vegetables in her kitchen. I've got a picture blown up of her in my kitchen, too, but for a different kind of inspirational purpose.

A tip: When ordering pizza, I like to put it on the radiator instead of in the fridge. It stays warm for days.

Kitchen Floor Tile

Instead of doing a regular ol' checkered floor, get some tiles and try some different approaches. They come in vinyl squares, and they don't have to be laid out on the floor in a checkered pattern. You can place them however you like—in a pattern that creates some type of picture, or any other design you want. You can also put these on the wall and on the ceiling for a really weird affect. Use contrasting colored tiles to write a message across the floor.

Punk Shui Recipes

This isn't just a design book; it's also a lifestyle book. I gathered a few of my favorite recipes that fit the punk shui taste—weird, maybe a little nasty, and definitely an acquired taste.

Peanuts in your Coca-Cola

I'm not a big cook, so this is my favorite. It requires very little prepping and no cooking. At the men's club in Hampshire, Tennessee, the town where I grew up, they used to drink Coke in old-fashioned bottles and put salted peanuts in it. Nobody in New York believes me—but this is one of the best tastes in the world. Warning: Do not do this with an alu-

minum can, because when you drink it, the nuts get caught on
the lip of the opening and don't come out.

Slut Sauce (sometimes known as Puttanesca)

Tomato sauce is the only recommended ingredient. Like
punk shui, there is not an exact formula for this sauce. Typically it's made to go over pasta, but that doesn't mean it can't
serve as soup. It's called slut sauce because, supposedly, the
whores (*puttana*) who began making this were very poor,
and just used whatever they had in their kitchens. If you have
these ingredients, or any others, of course, this is good shit.
Usually it doesn't include meat, either. I guess the sluts
couldn't afford the animal kind. Basically, throw all of your ingredients, whatever is not completely rotten in your refriger-
ator, into a pan, bring to a simmer for about five minutes, and
serve over whatever the hell you want.

The Eternal Pot of Stew (for a large gathering)

This is a recipe that I got from my client Steve Berman, one of my most beloved henchmen of alternative design and the founder of a punk shui offshoot called funk shui. (Most people in charge of a movement don't endorse those who come up with their own ideas and break away from the original flock of followers, but I am more generous and much cooler than most cult leaders.) Look for the funk shui manifesto to be published soon. Meanwhile, Berman gives us this recipe for your next punk or funk shui festivity.

* 170 onions
* 120 carrots
* 80 sticks of celery
* 50 pounds potatoes
* A whole lotta beef, the more the merrier (leave out when serving vegans ... or burn it to a crisp and just tell them it's wood-chip stew)

★Fresh parsley, basil and oregano

★Salt and pepper to taste

Prepare all ingredients and place in an extremely large crock pot (or a lavatory receptacle if you must, but be sure that it is fully heat-tempered ceramic or it may crack).

Bring to a slow simmer and replenish as needed forever and ever. This stew must never simmer below 160 degrees Fahrenheit. Vegans wishing to file a complaint can do so by sending themselves a self-addressed stamped envelope, to ensure that it will remain in the utmost confidentiality.

Bathrooms: Punk Shui Convenience

You can begin punk shui'ing your bathroom by removing some of (not all) convenience items, or changing their placement. For example, if you have a mirror over your sink—you can move it to the floor. That doesn't really mean we want to take away all convenience.

124 Punk Shui

Some is needed. For instance, I put a comb stand in my sink.

The comb stand itself is a cactus. This presents a different kind of un-conventional kind of convenience. Convenience in punk shui usually comes with a compromise or sacrifice. Another thing I like to do in my bathroom is to make sure I have something to read when I do my business. It's nice to have a few magazines:

This three-foot-stack of magazines is precarious, but convenient. When you reach for a mag, you're never sure if the entire stack is going to topple over on you.

Shower Exposure

Enough about convenience—let's get back to hardcore punk shui in the bathroom. You can take function out of the bathroom in different ways. Lose your shower curtain and see how it feels. This is about throwing privacy out the window. There's something liberating about being in the open, naked, splashing water on the floor.

I made my own wooden shower curtain that doesn't really do a lot for privacy or keeping water off the floor.

A tip: If you want to push the inconvenience to another level, put your shampoo and soap outside the shower so you have to reach for them. And try not to fall.

Get creative with the décor. How have you decorated your bathroom in the past? Let me guess—you went to Target and found a green bath mat to match your green shower curtain and green toothbrush holder—very original. Think about it. Besides going without a shower curtain, what else can make your bathroom a totally unique place? Maybe you hang your toothbrushes from the ceiling with floss, maybe you decide your bath mat looks better on the wall. Try some different things in the bathroom, and see where it takes you. And remember, all of those bathroom "accessories" they make you think you need (and need to be color-coordinated) are just extra things to spend your dollars on and replace your creative instincts with.

Detachable Toilet Seat

This is for all those guys who are sick of putting down the seat when they have a date in the house. When she needs it, it's resting on the toilet paper rack.

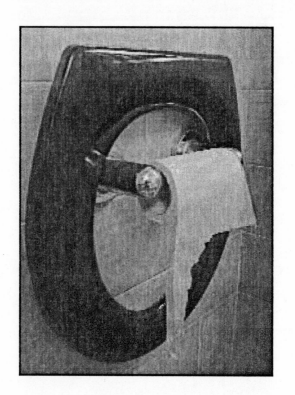

130 Punk Shui

Punk Shui Just-in-Case Emergency Kit

I have a collection of rusty razors I keep in my shower, so that just in case I'm having one of those mornings and I just want to end it, these babies are on standby.

Safety in the Home

We know that legally we need to cover this area, especially with all of the risky suggestions we have in this book. That's why we've provided the following special section for this purpose. Everything you need to know to be safe is in this section.

8

Colors, Accessories, and multimedia

Color and the Man

When I was waiting to begin a lecture for a group of art students, Tim Dubinsky, a big fan of punk shui, who was organizing the lecture, showed me a book he had just received. It's a book of colors that is released every year from some pain-in-the-ass government agency. In this book are the colors that the government forecasts will be used in design and fashion for the upcoming year. *How scary is that shit?*

By the end of the lecture I had almost forgotten about the book, but at the last minute in my closing remarks I saw it and picked it up and told the group I would be damned if I used any of those colors again.

I guarantee you that Pottery Barn, IKEA, and other chain stores will be showcasing these colors in the coming year, and continuing, with the government, to make our artistic and design choices for us. As the unknowing consuming public, we become sheep with basic design and artistic choices.

These days, if people don't have a lot of money, and they need basic furniture, they go to Pier 1, Target, or IKEA. What begins happening is that no one cultivates their own individual taste. No one takes the time to figure out what they really and truly want to do in their pad. Everyone's style and basic home design begins morphing into whatever style the leading retailer has decided on for that particular "season." Across the country, people begin mutating into robots with the same homogeneous aesthetic tendencies until we all look like we live in the apartment from *Friends*. It begins to matter less and less what *you* want, what *you* like, what aesthetic fits *your* personal lifestyle and moods or where you live. You could be in New York or in a suburb in Kansas, and you both have the same lime green "hip" mod sofa. Because that's all you can afford, you get duped into thinking this is all you can use to furnish your home. And, hey, everybody else is doing it.

As we've said several times so far, punk shui is inexpensive and easy, and it retains your own individual taste and creativity. I'm guessing you'd rather have your artistic choices displayed in your home than some generic Swedish designer's work that is becoming the only choice for many.

Let's put it this way: Anybody who knows his nose from his ass is going to be more impressed with a repainted table from the Salvation Army than with some shit you ordered out of a catalog from IKEA. It's not about impressing people, but you get the point. That said, watch what colors you choose, and why you choose them. When you see a color you are drawn to, ask yourself, is it because it's been featured in every store window in your neighborhood, or is it because you really like it? Is it because you saw a commercial, or have you always liked booger green? Are you choosing color schemes that have been subliminally hammered into your head by advertising, or are you choosing them because they are what you want?

Institutionalize Yourself

Now that we've talked about how shitty government colors are, let's talk about how *institutional* colors can create some really cool sensory deprivation. Schools, prisons, and jails have definite color themes for very specific reasons. You might have noticed the institutional versions of grays, puke greens, pale orange and yellow, stale blues, dirty whites—colors that never really live up to the color they call themselves. Burdened by multiple coats of generic paint, these colors are not drab just because they didn't have money in the budget for hiring a fabulous interior designer. Behind their sullen, uninspiring hues, there is a deliberate, manipulative reason why they suck. They are meant to subdue and subjugate, basically to kill any outstanding character, artistic sensibilities, or rebellion. These colors are to institutionalize you as a person, while you're in that institution. They were designed with the benefit of the institution in mind—not the individual.

I don't know exactly why you'd want to use these government-dictated colors in your home—but why not? You can use these colors to dull your senses in one room, and in another you can do some explosive, creative stuff with color so that your senses are deprived in one room and overloaded in another. That's a special kind of high. Or you could make your whole apartment totally institutionalized and have your senses accosted when you leave. This might work if you're a sorry bastard who has a job you hate. This way, going to work will feel like getting out of prison (twisted, huh?).

Black and White

Since this book is in black and white, our section on color is a little limited. But one idea is to only use black and white in your home to re-create the feel of an old Hitchcock film. (You have to figure out when to listen to me, because I told you not to do themes.) If you go for this kind of thing, it's a great way to work in rusted tools and worn antiques.

Hats

This may sound weird, but I like to put hats on the walls and around the apartment. They're a great accessory to almost anything. You can

Acrylic on canvas, by Brian Ermanski.

put them on all sorts of strange things and people. It's pretty simple: you just put the hat on top of something, to give it extra character. I've got one on a fan and another on a globe in my apartment. They can be any kind of hat—strange, eccentric, or fun. The first thing people do is put on the hat and wear it around. It never fails. That's what I call interactive punk shui.

Sculpt That Shit (Not Feces)

Punk shui may be a little extreme and over the top for some people, but others like the idea of chaos and creativity and what it does for them, even in small ways. In such instances, when you don't necessarily want to punk shui out your entire home, sculptures can lend the feel of inspiring alternative design. You crazy freaks who are going whole-hog will dig it, too.

There is no real defining element in my sculpture, and I don't want to go so far as to categorize punk shui sculptures. I'll say this, though: Sculptures can be anything that takes up space and produces

creative energy in the environment. They serve as artistic reminders of an aesthetic of which some only need a small dose. For instance, you may have what's called a "normal apartment," but in the middle of your bedroom you have a whacked-out sculpture that you made using all your old *Star Wars* collector's items. Whatever the scenario, a sculpture can be a concentrated piece of punk shui aesthetic in a sea of normalcy—it can be your oasis or your demon, jarring you out of your boring existence. Just make sure it's original.

Punk shui sculpture is about giving another life to things that have already lived one life. Find the second, third, and fourth lives in your (or someone else's) furniture, possessions, or "garbage." If you have some clichéd idea that sculpture is limited to the traditional bronze bust—let go of that. Look around your apartment or home and see if anything looks tired and invites your creativity to bring it into its next life. You figure it out. There's no goofy how-to way to do sculpture. We can't do it for you. This is where you have to get inspired and do your own art—or buy mine (www.punkshui.net).

I will say that one way to get started is to put your least favorite object in the middle of the room. Another might be to go through your closet and use an appliance that hasn't worked for years as your

starting point. Maybe an outfit you used to wear years ago will inspire you. There are countless ways to start your own sculpture.

One of my favorite sculptures is a fan I found on the street. The cage was smashed in and didn't allow the blades to turn. I took off the cage and it works fine. The only thing you have to worry about is that if you get too close you could lose a finger—but that makes it a functioning sculpture and Perfect Punk Shui™.

Music

I personally find a lot of inspiration in a variety of different music. I'm down with punk music (I think that's obvious by now), but am inspired by all kinds of music. You can use music to help get your blood going when you work on your space, and to add energy to space.

My dad told me one time, "There's only two kinds of music. Good music and bad music."

Speaking of the good kind, one of my favorite musicians is Bob Dylan, because every time someone's tried to put a label on him, he's always changed up his game. For instance, the dude appeared in a Victoria's Secret ad! We can speculate all day long as to why (I have my theories), but, regardless, I think we can safely say we didn't see that one coming. Unlike most musical artists these days, he didn't give a shit about feeding fans what they thought they wanted. He did it his way. He always has a surprise, whether it's busting out with an electric guitar versus an acoustic one amid the protests of his fans, or selling panties.

I tell this story because the only quality I think is necessary when finding music to incorporate into your punk shui design is that the artist who created it be an example to you—maybe they went their own way, rebelling against the norm, or made some revolutionary music. That's the only quality I look for—be it punk, rock and roll, jazz, bluegrass—whatever. Just make sure the artist isn't a poser.

Sound Effects

The effect of sound on your energy, psyche, and atmosphere should be considered, regardless of what you're trying to accomplish in your home, and especially if you have nothing in particular to accomplish.

Figure out what it can add to your place. It's not about getting your same ol' CDs, records, or radio station and playing it loud, it's about experimenting with sounds you've never considered before and making them intrinsic to the atmosphere of a space.

When I began punk shui'ing regularly, I used to tune my antique radio to a station that was mostly static with intermittent voices. I would keep it like that constantly for a day, and then shut it off the next day. The relief and silence I felt was amazing. Suddenly I didn't mind the occasional car horns as I had before, and I actually noticed a rare silence between the sirens and people's shouts on the street outside my apartment.

Almost everywhere in the country there's a college station, and almost every college station has some guy or girl who stays up all night and plays weird, strange, monotonous music. I suggest taping one of those shows and using that as the background to chillin' out in your apartment. Whatever you're used to listening to—change it, and try some funky new crazy shit, even if it makes no sense at all and makes you want to pull your hair out. I have a client who has lasers on some of his thresholds. When you go through one of his doors and break the laser's beam, different sounds are activated. The main door to his apartment usually emits a high-pitched scream that sounds like someone is being murdered.

Making Sounds

Homemade instruments are cool to record for your pad. My client Si made a banjo out of a cookie tin and carved the neck. It's actually a fully functioning banjo, and makes some interesting sounds. He says, "I read a book that was about instrument making 'back on the farm' and how they used to make instruments out of gourds and cake boxes. I decided to try my hand and see what kind of sound it made. It sounds tin-like and Chinese."

One of my favorite ways to listen to a record is distorted through a guitar amplifier. All you do is take an old-school record player and hook it up to an amp and hit the distortion button. It'll make whatever you're listening to sound really different. It distorts the entire sound, even lyrics, and gives every record a punk shui vibe. You could make classical music sound like rock and roll. Si actually did that and recorded it and then used that recording as an instrument in a song.

Another punk shui enthusiast, Guy, and his friends play nonid-iomatic and experimental music, meaning no set characteristics define his style, nor is there anything in particular that distinguishes him as belonging to a specific group. At the last show they played, Guy actually played a bass with hemostats (otherwise known as roach clips), crouched down on all fours underneath a bed sheet with a giant record glued to his back. The singer, Jeff, played a chellar (a cross between a cello and a guitar), and the third member of the band played a toy piano that was wired up to some 1980s-era electronics. These types of experiments are great ways to entertain and give you an idea of the kind of music that can change the whole climate of your pad. Out of the typical shitty top-forty box you go, and into a whole other dimension, where not only are different design techniques created, but also the types of sounds you might listen to regularly. As Guy has discovered, you can leave the confines of music genres and escape to punk shui land, where anything goes.

Another client of mine started recording some really weird sounds to play when he would punk out his apartment. He would literally put nails on the chalkboard, play records backward, and have a slew of other knocking, clanking noises that were altogether uncomfortable. He then would play them at low levels when people came over to see what their reactions would be like. When asked by them, "What the hell is that sound?" He would reply, "I don't know what you're talking about."

Multimedia Punk Shui

Using TV monitors in your apartment is a dynamic way to utilize visual art in design. Jim Budman, the owner of the studio in Soho where some of my work is on display, is a pioneer in multimedia video art. He has made a habit of taping everything for over two decades now. He has archives containing years of videos. Often the videos are of his own life and of artists making art. He ties time together with the archives by using his past and present videos intermittently. As he says:

> What has been created is an extensive archive ... we are starting to use the present tapes ... and pull some of the present past (yesterday or last week) and play it back on monitors and also pull some of the past archives (could be from a few years back) and we're starting to mix the footage to create

a documentary. We're using the past archive, the present archive, and the present shooting...In the studio I have monitors running with different footage and in many cases it's unedited...It just runs. Sometimes people will come up on one monitor and another...and I always try to shoot something off the monitors when I'm shooting in present time. Let's say Josh is at the studio doing something, but at the same time he may be on monitor, sitting on the punk shui couch.

He videotapes his own video installations so you see layer after layer. In a way, he's giving each video a different perspective and another life, and ultimately giving the viewer another layer of voyeurism. Just as we give old furniture or objects new lives, Jim gives his footage another context

By using video, the atmosphere in the studio is taken to another level beyond the painting and sculpture, and it becomes about the interaction of the artists *and* their art, on tape. It is a fascinating way to use art and energy. Using interactive video this way can change the fabric of everyone's experience through visual stimulation. And, as Jim says, "It is what it is."

You could set up a projector to run old home movies or videos you've shot, projected on your wall. Just like in the studio, this form of visual art will add another layer to your design.

Organic Touches

Plants are really awesome things to use when punk shui'ing your apartment. If you use vine-like plants in particular, you can place them so that they break into different spaces. This plant was put in a picture frame, but it breaks the confines of the frame with its vines. These are also good plants to hang over your bed where your head usually goes. Cacti are great, too, thanks to their prickles and their harsh nature. Sometimes I'll put large cactuses in my clients' hallways so they have to move slowly and deliberately around it without pricking them-selves.

For one of my clients, Rhonda, we put a tree in the middle of her living room floor. It was around four feet high and she situated all of the couches and chairs around it. Another of my clients, Katie, has been doing punk shui with her dead Christmas tree. It's a few feet high, in a pot. After Christmas it died, and now she's used it in various

places in her apartment. Talk about having the Christmas spirit all year long.

How weird can you get with vegetation? That's the question you need to ask yourself if you're inclined to add it to your pad.

Aquariums and Terrariums

Don't underestimate what you can do with aquariums and terrariums. One client of mine had a huge aquarium with a ton of fish, and put her old TV set in it. Another client made tunnels using beer cans through the rocks on the bottom for a bottom-feeding fish to swim through.

I have another client, Betsy, who put a huge terrarium in the middle of her living room floor with a giant black snake in it. She said, "It was such a trip watching people come into the room and check out Lacy [the snake]. Some people got really excited, and others were just freaked out. We used the top of the terrarium as a coffee table. I think she likes the constant company."

Another client of mine, Mike, puts his boa constrictor's terrarium on a stand above the head of his bed in his room. As he goes to sleep, he knows the snake is coiled above him.

Pets

Snakes aren't the only pets that can be incorporated into punk shui. My client Beth has two cats named Buster and Flynn. She dresses them up regularly in little spiked collars and punk T-shirts and allows them to eat with her at her table. Beside her plate she puts their bowl. She has made her pool table into a little kitty palace where they sleep and play. It's a little weird, but cool. And the cats love the extra attention. They have almost no rules in her house. Her guests get kind of weirded out—but some people love it. She's living the way she wants to, according to no rules or protocol with her pets. That's punk shui.

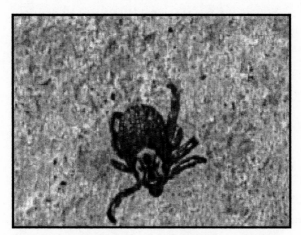

This is a pet tick that I had for a few days and didn't even know it.

Accessories Should Inspire:
Find Your Kachina Doll

As you collect accessories for your home, one of the qualities to be on the lookout for is something that inspires you. Try to shake off the clichéd views of inspiration, because when you get down to it, inspiration is not some warm and fuzzy impressionistic painting print that you got at Barnes & Noble—it can be gritty, nasty, weird, and completely unique to you.

When asked what inspires him in his pad, Mike Watt responded, "My kachina dolls and my Pettibons." Watt is referring to his friend Raymond Pettibon's art. Every time he gets a chance, he acquires a new kachina doll. Kachina dolls are uniquely weird pieces of art because they were originally created by the Hopi Indians. They are said to have originated in the San Francisco Peaks of Arizona, and are meant to assist with the growing season and symbolize fertility, good harvest, long life, and all that good stuff. Sometimes they represent dead spirits. When you look at these pictures, it's easy to see they have a strange quality to them. "They are my jury . . . they dance when

we have earthquakes [and they] help make me sane." Who knew?

Maybe your kachina dolls are a collection of old records or pieces of scrap metal or destroyed furniture or different kinds of lamps. Maybe you're like one of my clients, and are crazy about maimed teddy bears. Whatever it is, don't limit yourself. As Watt's shelves of kachina dolls expand, so does the energy in his pad.

9

Out of your Box

Using punk shui to break through the malaise and everyday boredom of normalcy does not have to be limited to your apartment or house. Not in the least. I actually decided to have a punk shui art opening on the street and invite some friends. I told everyone that came by that I had placed this large Dumpster of rock and rubble on the street, and I was paying $1,000 a day to keep it there and observe reactions. This, of course, was a total lie. It was a dumpster placed in front of my house by the New York City

Rubble-Placing Department. I had a bunch of people hang out around it, as they might at a gallery open house. Check it out.

Here are some responses from the attendees of the opening:

"I just love being on the cutting edge of art." —Anonymous tourist

"The dirt and rubble of the dumpster was absolutely breathtaking." —Anonymous NYC sculptor

"It's there, it's just there. Totally unbelievable." —Anonymous art critic

"This is a total load of bullshit." —Anonymous NYC "interior decorator"

The exhibit was a classic example of punk shui contradictions, lack of rules, and basic nonsensical reasoning, while proving a point all the same (I'll let you figure out what that point was).

Taking punk shui out of the home and into the world is a great way to expand the effects. It's good stuff. In this chapter we're going explore punk shui's ability to work in other physical environments besides just your pad. Taking punk shui into your work, your ride, your travel style, your yard, or even your own business is a way to constantly expand your own boundaries.

The Cube

For those who have to deal with the misery of working in a cubicle every day, I think you'll agree that it is an environment that would greatly benefit from some punk shui therapy. Shit, I hate that word "therapy." I mean punk shui treatment. Damn, I hate that one, too. How about punk shui *stuff?* Much better.

Frank works in an office and has a cubicle. Frank hates his job. He has a strong distaste for his boss. He hates the sandwich shop where he goes to buy a sensible turkey sandwich every afternoon. If he feels like getting crazy, he buys Twinkies for dessert. Every morning Frank wakes up and thinks, *I hate my cubicle at work, and that's where I'm going.* Frank is not yet ready to shed these awful chains of misery. But he does want to do his job on his terms. This is where punk shui comes in.

Frank tackled that cubicle with a vengeance. He cut holes in the "walls," he tacked up rock posters and put a dead plant on top of his computer. He stenciled the words LIVE ANIMALS on one of the walls. He set up speakers on top of the file cabinets. He made that mother fucking cubicle his own—and sometimes that's what we need to do in this world—make a piece of where we dwell or work our own. His comment on the makeover:

> The message working in a cubicle sent to my brain was, "You are a droid, you are like everyone else, you are in the rat race." Now, that message made me want to quit my job and drive off into the sunset to god knows what, but I need my effing job. So, even though punk shui can't change that, when I get up every morning and go to work, at least I am reminded, as I send memos, file, and stand in line at the copier, that I am not an effing droid. At least now I can look out of the jagged holes that I cut into my cubicle and think, "Everything is malleable." And in the back of my mind there is always the possibility that, thanks to my destruction of company property, I will get fired.

By the way, if you don't want to do this because you're afraid to get fired, maybe you're in the wrong job.

Another client of mine, Ralph, got these nasty e-mails from his boss all the time. He began printing the e-mails, copying them, and enlarging them 500 percent on the copier. When he had done that, he

would cut out various letters and words from the copies and add them to his cubicle walls until there was a giant, distorted, and freakish-looking collage surrounding him. Everyone he worked with would know when the boss was being an asshole because there would be an addition to the collage.

Punk It Further at Work

Punking out your work style doesn't even have to be design-based; it can be conceptual, lifestyle rebellion. Besides just decorating your office walls or cube, punk it out further—post an out-of-office reply when you're not out of the office, or screw around with your identity and tell everyone you changed your name to Ricky the Ranger or Fuck Face. See how it feels. Send a company-wide e-mail making your name change official, and see what everyone says. Why not? Changing your boundaries means changing the way people see you, speak to you, and interact with you. Change your "look" and wear a Halloween mask to work one day, or dress like a woman if you're a man, or like a man if you're a woman.

Try not using a calendar for a week, try to forget what day it is, don't schedule appointments, just tell people to drop by and see what it feels like to banish the meaning of a schedule from your life. As far as clocks go, stare at the sun for a while if you want to know what time it is. Go ahead and let people know that "you don't do meetings," and treat the water cooler gossip as if you didn't understand the

English language. When someone offers you the latest office-gossip dirt, just say, "*No habla inglés.*"

Change the world you live in by changing yourself and people's perception of you (and your perception of your life) one punk shui move at a time. As soon as we are confronted with the unexpected, a whole other dimension of our lives takes its turn. We become freer and less predictable by the minute, and I can promise we will have a lot fewer dull moments.

Punk Shui Whips (That's "Cars" for Those Not Down with It)

It's fun to get crazy with your car, truck, or golf cart. I had one client who cut a hole in his dashboard so he could put a flower box into it. Another took the passenger seat out of his van and put in a beanbag chair. Another painted a mural on her car and pimped out the sound system so that she had a speaker on the roof for when she wanted to blast music.

Ruth, one of my clients, grows wheatgrass in the back of her car.

This is my ride. It's only five inches tall, but I'm cool with that.

That's where she gets the most light regularly. She also painted a couple of the passenger doors different colors. "I'm always able to pick out my car in a crowded parking lot—it doesn't look like every other person's car. I'm so sick of the lack of character vehicles have, in general. It makes me feel like your average, everyday consumer. I need to feel like I dance to a different tune."

This is the coolest ice cream truck I've ever seen. He has big monster truck tires on the back and he pumps out his own music all day long while he cruises. He has all of these images of women all over the truck, the kind you'd see on an eighteen-wheeler's mud flaps. There's nothing that dude from *Pimp My Ride* could do to this truck that hasn't already been done except put an LED on the gas cap.

Mile-High Punk Shui

I figured out some cool ways to get some space on planes. I have a turban I wear sometimes, after skipping a few days of washing. When I go this route, on takeoff I usually babble incoherently for a while, as if in a trance. After this, I'm able to stretch out on the surrounding seats as the other passengers find elsewhere to sit. (That's what they get for stereotyping.) A little tip: if you take the aisle-seat flotation device and lean it against the wall, just kick your feet up and you've got yourself a punk shui La-Z-Boy.

When I'm out and about in the great wide world, I find the sterile aesthetic of hotel rooms repulsive. I like to punk shui them so I can feel at home. Sometimes I put the mattress on the floor, one time I

slept in the tub, and another time I took down all of the pictures of grass dunes and flowers and put them in the closet and then put some of my own art on the walls.

How much you punk shui your hotel room can depend on your budget, too. You don't want to start painting on the wall or sawing the couch in half if you don't have the money to pay for it when the hotel manager finds out. Jail is for the diehards.

There are different kinds of hotels to consider if you feel the same way I do about the décor and cardboard sheets. My friend Brian Ermanski, who is a painter, has been asked to paint a room at the San Francisco Hotel des Arts, in the French Quarter. The hotel invited emerging artists to paint and/or design different rooms. The result is a totally unique experience for every room that's painted. Each artist paints the atmosphere of the room, taking it over. The hotel also has an art gallery that features a number of up-and-coming artist's work. For a totally different experience, check it out. It beats a typical hotel, with the crappy pictures of flowers, sea gulls, and sand dunes. It's also a great idea to support businesses like this that go a different route and try to give their guests something special and artistic.

Animal House

If you're in college, or want to pretend you are, punk shui can definitely complement the learning and/or partying years. Taking punk

shui into your dorm environ can be fun, especially if you find a group of people willing to punk shui out a whole dorm. One group of people in particular comes to mind. I won't name the school, and I'll call the group the Math Club. (They are now "grown up" and somewhat "respectable"—those assholes. It's a tragedy.) One of the highlights of their college years was the pair of testicles from a cadaver in a jar of formaldehyde on top of the TV in the commons room (it was stolen by a premed student from the biology department). As I told you, sculptures and art can be made from anything. That includes human remains, bone, and other dead organic materials.

The Math Club enjoyed riding motorcycles down the halls of the dormitory, leaving tire tracks on a few of the walls. These boys (not many girls participated) used blowtorches and hammers on the doors to their rooms to create the "pillaged" look they were going for. They also sponsored events in the yard of the dorm in which there was a kiddy pool of grain alcohol and a Slip 'n Slide that could only be used by buck-naked participants.

I could go on and on about the frontiers of punk shui aesthetics these guys forged (and the various times they took trips to the dean's office). One of the main things I took away from my experience with these guys was the fearlessness they had in their living quarters. No boundaries, no fear, and the consistent raising of the bar put them into the Punk Shui Hall of Fame.

Punk Shui Yard

A yard, if you have one, can pose some interesting opportunities. I have a cabin in Tennessee where I keep a Shooting Car. For those who don't know, this is a car that doesn't run anymore, which my friends and I shoot at. Call it white trash if you must—I call it punk shui.

I also have some sculptures I made out of mannequins that I place in varying poses (some X-rated, some not) when I have parties.

To add to the strange mix of yard deco, I have an upside-down Jacuzzi. Whenever anyone asks what it is, I say it's a time machine. And you probably won't believe it, but a lot of girls think that's cool. One even believed me.

Large yard art can be kickass. You can do things in your yard that you can't in your house, because of the limitations on space.

Here is another punk shui yard:

Let your yard go. Don't cut the grass. By the time you have a mini-jungle out there, it can give your house a deserted look, which actually deters door-to-door salespeople.

You can also decorate trees in your yard. Making sculptures in the

yard can change the whole vibe of your house when you come and go. It also serves as an introduction to anyone who drives by. They don't even have to come into your pad to catch a whiff of this punk shui vibe.

Maura of Punk Rock Aerobics told us, "I am so happy to even

have a yard. Actually, an old friend of mine has had a ten-foot van parked in my yard for four years—the van doesn't work, but it remains in the yard as a monument to when he toured with his band in the nineties. It is now covered in mold, and it dawned on me that if he doesn't tow it away soon, I may have to work with nature to turn it into an enormous Chia Pet."

Punk Shui Bleeds into Business

I would like to say something to those of you who are freaked out about leaving the shelter of a cushy job or a crappy corporation. Chances are you're not being thanked, you're getting burnt out, and you don't necessarily have creative ownership. If you're not happy—let's face it, folks, what the fuck are you doing?

To all of you poor schmucks who dread your jobs, bitch about them, and generally lead a pretty unhappy existence, this is your chance to punk it out.

Punk it out! Think past what you are *used* to doing every day, and think forward to a realm in which no rules apply, work doesn't have to be "work," and you can greet each morning with the relief that you're not going to work for, with, or around jerks. Breaking out of your routine and traditional concepts of lifestyle choices, especially ones you didn't consciously choose, is more than designing a place you can live with, it's about creating an atmosphere, be it work or home, that suits you—and only you. Not what your parents said you should do, not what your friends are doing, and certainly not what your boss expects. This is about you.

One of my clients, Wayne, said of punking out his career and going into business for himself,

> When I met Josh, I had been working as a writer for a company for a few years. I was doing great, I had a promotion, money was better, and I had thought that was what I wanted, but once I got it, it wasn't all that great. The web of corporate BS seemed like it was miles long and I'd never escape if I stayed there. After spending some time punk shui'ing my apartment, and hearing Josh's rhetoric, I said, "Screw the job. I'll never really know who I am until I go my own way." Since then, I can't imagine going back. Now I make my living with my own business, doing my own writing and sculpture. Some-

times I make a little cash on the side selling pot to cancer patients.

There are plenty of people who have figured out how to take their work and refusal to conform out of their apartments and into the their businesses. I'll introduce you to a few people who have figured out how to have a business that works for them, and defies a lot of the norms that are so prevalent in the modern corporate company. These are the people who have figured out how to work outside the box—rather than just *think* outside the box. I hope their efforts will inspire you to do the same.

I don't really do aerobics, but these guys sound like they're having fun. Maura Jasper and Hilken Mancini wrote a book and have a business that is centered around punk rock aerobics. Who the fuck knew? They teach classes in the Boston area and not only use punk music, but punk philosophy and aesthetics. As they say about punk in their book, *Punk Rock Aerobics,* "Punk makes it possible for anyone to be a rock star—you don't have to be able to play guitar or sing to perform." 'Nuff said. They used this approach in their business, defying rules, the norm, and traditional business practice. As they said, "We had no model, no experience. It was DIY all the way." They run a business based on things they have fun doing—now that's a revolutionary concept, especially for those in this society who feel that work has to be work. Work can be play, PRA demonstrates.

Based in Boston, PRA has attracted quite a few fans. You've got to love a business that lures people in by asking, "Are you not immune to the occasional Joe Strummer–style Air Guitar Jump?" Rock on.

Another example of some folks who figured out how to create and work in a space they couldn't find in traditional businesses are Shawna Kenny and her husband, Rich, who recently opened a bookstore named Rebel Books in Wilmington, North Carolina. "Our approach is completely grassroots," she told us. "The whole reason for starting the store comes from a punk rock philosophy. If I want to change something, I do it myself. I was going all over the country to get the books and art I wanted, and I realized that I would create a place where I lived to get the kinds of things I wanted." Basically, she decided to offer alternatives besides the chain bookstores and yuppified art galleries. She based her vision of her business on "accepting imperfection," which is a really powerful idea when you think of it in relation to the way other businesses in the country operate.

They also relied on alternative/punk rock practice to get the word out about their store; they made flyers and T-shirts and distributed them without paying the typical advertising channels. They've gotten a lot of press for it, too.

My clients Kyle and Stephen have begun a business based on getting vintage clothes from Goodwill, Salvation Army, or the junk store, modifying them in different ways and putting them up for sale on eBay. They are making a business out of giving things a second and third life. Originally Kyle worked for a typical company, and now he has his own. I asked him a few questions:

Is fashion design art or business?

"When I first worked in corporate fashion, I was shocked at what passed for creativity and design. The entire industry is based on copying someone's ideas that were copied from someone else that were copied from someone else and presenting them as original. It was frustrating when the head designer would hand me a garment purchased in a store in Florence or Paris and ask me to send it to the agent in Hong Kong for copying...the pressure to make profits limits true artistic expression for most."

What inspires you?

"I was always inspired by what was meant to impress the least. For fashion inspiration, I carefully study people who can't afford to shop. In their hapless and chaotic lives they still find a way to express themselves. Even though they wear what they found in the trash, there is elegance to the total insignificance of fashion in their lives."

What are you working on now?

"One of my most exciting projects is Dumpster Chic, the couture clothing that I design from salvaged home furnishings. One of the principles of punk shui is the deconstruction and repurposing of discarded objects into art. The once-subservient kitchen drapes become a beautiful couture gown; this transformation from utilitarian object into art is exhilarating."

You discussed the business of fashion. How do you thing punk shui intersects with business?

"If there is anything that needs to be deconstructed today, it is the American corporation. I am not suggesting dismantlement; punk shui motivates the deconstruction and repurposing of objects and ideas to be viewed in a new light. American industrial corporations could use this philosophy to revitalize their flagging revenues and profits. Imagine if General Motors deconstructed the concept of the automobile and repurposed it for environmental protection."

What advice would you give to someone trying to explore their own creative punk shui philosophy in business?

"Don't build a business, tear one down."

Punk Shuied Business
of Punk Shui

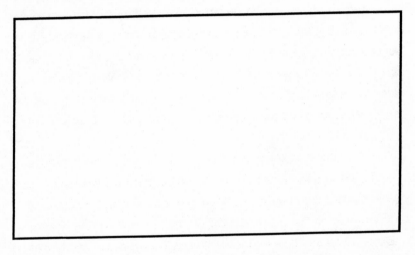

As for me, I try to focus on making art with each business venture, rather than making a "brand," "look," or overall "image." If I made those my goals, I would immediately be added to the league of the thousands of other designers struggling to make money and "make their name in the business." Screw that. As my client Kyle said above, building a business is for suckers, doing what you love is for punk shui enthusiasts. It's also about broadening the basic philosophy of business in general, of deconstructing capitalism and the very foundation of what has gotten us, as a society, so enthused about all of the accessories of business, like mass marketing, advertising, bullshitting, and trying in general to get people to buy your idea over others, which inevitably turns into trying to get everyone to think the way you do, rather than think for themselves. That said, I try to focus on the art rather than the money, the inventive thought rather than repeating a look, and the outrageous choice rather than consistency.

For example, instead of making five hundred business cards at a printer, with the same design and "brand" for my business, I make each business card individually on my antique typewriter. It's not the most efficient way to do it, I'll grant you, but that's not the point. They're all one of a kind and designed differently. Each card could be considered a piece of art, so when you give it to someone, they may really appreciate it and they keep it longer than they might otherwise. It may take a while to make these, but it's usually well worth the time. Anyway, with my business, it's not about mass production or about how many people on the street have a card.

Here are some of the things that distinguish my business style from your typical business practices:

* ✳ I sure as hell didn't write a business plan.
* ✳ I pay most of my employees with cigarettes.
* ✳ I usually pay my taxes a year or two behind.
* ✳ In my business, going public means streaking down Wall Street.

Punk It Further: Your Business

If you're thinking about opening your own business, or even getting paid to do something on the side, outside of a formal job, open your mind to the different possibilities. Think in terms of what you can do, instead of what you're "qualified" to do. It's a lot more fun. I mean, would you have ever considered that someone could open a business based on *punk rock aerobics?* Maybe you've always wanted the freedom of doing your own thing, but you don't think you have experience or know-how—so what? People dupe you into thinking you need their product or service, even if you don't—that's business. I know some guys who opened a business that specializes in hanging flyers—the simplest thing you can do! Maybe you've always wanted to do singing telegrams—slap up a web page and turn on the OPEN sign in the window. The only limits are what you perceive to be the boundaries of a traditional business. As soon as you begin to tear those down, you create your own.

10

Socialize with Punk Shui

What is this, amateur hour? Punk shui's the best thing to happen to social events since bootie dancing. If you can't have fun at a punk shui party, it's probably because you got drunk way too early. Or maybe you didn't get drunk late enough.

—DJ Casco

If you put punk shui into your party, you'll get awesome results, some good and probably some you didn't exactly expect. These parties can be used to get people out of their normal behavior patterns and rank boredom with one another, and into more interesting settings, creativity and a good time. To throw punk shui parties, you have to extract yourself from all of the traditional party methods.

Party Tips: Turning It Inside Out

Many of us have it ingrained in our minds that to be a great host we have to have good manners and make sure our guests are happy. With a punk shui party, the opposite is true. I have clients who don't even identify themselves as the host throughout the whole party. They enjoy it a hell of a lot more, too, because they don't have to be "on." Here are a few simple things to get you started and dismantle preconceptions you may have about throwing a party.

* Don't greet your guests or identify yourself as the host when they arrive at the party.
* Don't supply beverages or food.
* If you do want to supply beverages, keep them at room temperature and let your guests seek out the

beer in cases or boxes, tap the keg, mix the drinks, and go get ice.

* Take the labels off liquor bottles—the fun is in the mystery.
* Let people fix their own food—put out a grill or some pans and some veggies or a choice meat (Spam, hot dogs, or other delicacies), and let them go to town.
* Don't supply silverware or napkins.
* Put together a mixed CD of the most uncomfortable sounds you can find, and blare them from your stereo.

Think hard. What do you immediately think you have to do when people visit or you throw a party? Now do the opposite, or don't do anything at all. Become the anti-host and reinvent how you entertain—that, in and of itself, will be entertainment.

Party Don'ts

You're going to have rethink what you thought was awesome party event planning. Check out these punk shui party don'ts:

- beer pong
- body shots
- beer funnels
- keg stands
- drinking games
- basically anything you did at parties in college (besides sex)

Strange Gatherings

When I consult people on PS parties, I try to get them to do things they've never done before, from the most basic level, like deconstructing that obligatory-host shit, to throwing parties that really put them and their guests in a completely different element. One of my clients worked at a software company and felt that a lot of his co-workers were really a little uptight. Workwise, he felt suffocated by the conservatism of some of his computer-geek co-workers. He was sick of going to a job where the only things anyone did all day were talk about writing programs and make homophobic jokes. I helped him arrange to have a cross-dressing party for his co-workers. How did he get them to attend? Well, he told them that his sister was friends with a bunch of models from *Top Model,* that they would be there, and this was one of the trends in New York parties. Most of them hadn't been laid in quite some time, so they decided to go for it. They showed up in the most hilarious outfits you've ever seen. Most of them had so little fashion sense anyway that their posing as women didn't help things. When the models didn't show up, they had a few drinks and actually started to like their outfits. The next thing they knew, Steve and Ted from accounting were hooking up in the bathroom. What's the moral? If you help your friends break out of their molds, you'll have a great party, and a lot to talk about the next day.

Another way to spice up the party is to offer free drinks to anyone wearing underwear only. It always speeds up the action.

Disrupting the Quiet Desperation

We all know the different types of parties. Sometimes everyone sits facing each other and, depending on seating arrangements and the amount of alcohol consumed, you are forced to make polite conversation, like, "So, what do you do?" or, "Where do you live?" or, "I went to this incredible exhibit and I found so-and-so's stuff soo————". Blah, blah, blah. Of course, there's the dinner party get-together where everyone compliments the food, even if it sucks, and eats and drinks politely and sits beside people they're told to sit beside in some sort of demented seating arrangement that the host has concocted. If you're single, you may be seated beside someone the host hopes you will fall madly in love with so you aren't a third or fifth wheel anymore.

There are different ways to entertain and interact, and they don't have anything to do with those obnoxious, theme-based parties that feature some type of elaborate treasure hunt some bored woman and/or gay man has cooked up because he/she wants to be nominated hostess of the year. They don't demand wearing costumes, unless the guests want to. Screw fondue, potluck, or any other theme-based, Tupperware-derived gatherings. All of these sorry-ass attempts to reinvent parties that come from glossy magazines make my stomach turn. I always end up drinking too much to numb the pain until I can excuse myself.

Aren't you tired of the same ol' shit—the quiet desperation that lingers behind empty chatter, meaningless flirting, cheesy BS, and waking up in the morning feeling like an asshole because you got drunk *again* (by the way, that's not the part that I think sucks) because you were bored by the party and that was the only way you knew to have a good time. LAME. Now, this is by no means a therapy book, a self-help book, or any kind of cure-all, but if you try some different stuff, it will shake your preconceptions (you poor schmuck) and your quiet desperation to its very core. And if you're lucky, it will do more than just shake and shock you, it will inspire you to lead a more interesting existence. Unfortunately, I'm unable to quantify that because it's different for everybody. Get inspired and figure it out by yourself.

Of course, you might be one of those people who actually *like* vapid themes, grain alcohol in their tub, or, for godsakes, a board game in the middle of their party as the big highlight. If you are one of these people, you are to desist reading immediately and go back to the other side.

Seating Arrangements

I bag on theme parties, but a little arranging isn't bad. By turning the couch and chairs in different directions, effing up the typical "mingling" setup in which everyone's turned awkwardly to face people they don't want to talk to, you can create some cool situations. Lose all of the chairs and furniture and put some really strange stuff in their places. By putting sculptures where the seats normally go, you can give people some weird stuff to lean on and/or talk about.

One of my friends likes to hire actors to interact with the guests without telling anyone. Usually the actors are really effing weird. It's a little more original than hiring a stripper. You never know who's an actor or who's just a guest. I guess that's a little close to real life.

It's Not What You Have at Your Party—It's Who

To have a different kind of party you have to have different kinds of people. As so many entertainment books and gurus say, it's not about what's on the table or in people's hands, it's about who is there. I happen to agree with the gurus on this one. I had one client who was tired of inviting the same ol' people to her parties, weekend after weekend, occasion after occasion. We decided to find some new people. How did we do this? Well, part of what was boring about her parties was that she always knew who was coming. It was getting tired. So, rather than just pick a new group of people to invite, we decided to allow people to invite themselves. She made some flyers that advertised her party, but she said specifically, "If you're tired of the same ol' party—this one will be different. This is not a meat market, there will be no trendy band, and if you are a poser, do not even consider coming. Be prepared to attend a party like you've never been to before. And BYOB&YOB. Bring Your Own Booze and Your Own Brain." She included the date, time, location, and so on, and braced herself after she put the flyers up around her neighborhood. Upon my recommendation, she even arranged for a van of people to come over from the local mental institution. Total strangers filtered into her house, some early, some really late, and in general she had a great and freaky time meeting people she didn't know, especially the kinds of characters that respond to a flyer like that. If you're tired of the same group, the same digs, and the same routine, try to think outside the box and see what happens at your next party.

Make Art at the Party

One of my friends, Martin, has some awesome parties where he has the guests put together art during the party. At one of these he decided to decorate his walls—or, rather, have his guests decorate his walls. He provided some broken mirrors, rusty tools, paints, spray paint, and some old pieces of furniture to be bashed, unlimited alcohol, and other choice party favors, and told everyone to go crazy. They did.

I ended up with a one of a kind design on my walls, and a fuzzy memory of who did what. At first some folks were really calculated about how they did things. They might try to make a specific design with paints or something. As the night wore on, some people got more into what they were doing and got super elaborate with designs. One I really like is a snake that runs the length of the molding on the ceiling, made out of broken mirror, wood, paint and sequins.

Not a bad deal—you get your place macked out and you get to have a kickin' party. At another party I went to, thrown by a guy named Fred, everyone began spontaneously painting all the walls in his house. It was a great party; we took some choice substances and had a ball.

Party Planning Is for Anal-Retentive Freaks

One of the things I would caution—don't make the party a decorating "theme" party. Just have it there, and if people partake, cool, and if

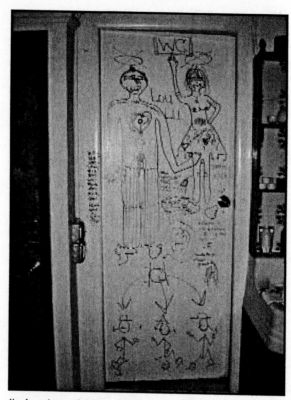

Here's a picture of the door that Brian and I did at a party one night.

they don't, cool. When I get some kind of e-mail or invite to a party and it's all mapped out, it makes me want to gag, and I rarely attend. Parties that happen in an easy, embrace-anything-that-comes-your-way approach are the best ones, anyway. Don't be an effing party planner. Every time I run into one of these posers, I feel sorry for them. With every theme-based plan they make, with every RSVP they request, and with every seating chart they put together, they are trying to control events, the guest list, and their own happiness. I know what you're thinking, that I'm sleeping with a therapist, or that I am intimately acquainted with one. Sorry, no—I don't think I'm reading too much into this. It's a sick habit some people get caught up in, so watch it that you don't become a party planner. We all want to hear "(*Insert your name here*) throws the kickass-est parties," but that's not how to do it.

That's when you've got to watch for the infamous ego, which inevitably makes you way too self-conscious, worried, and uptight. The ego is the part of the brain overused by the enemy (those who try to enforce any rule whatsoever on you at any time). The ego wants to control, and the ego is totally insecure. The ego is what punk shui seeks to ignore and take out of the driver's seat.

The ego is what's worried about controlling and manipulating the energy around you, worried about throwing the best party, worried about what people are going to think about you, worried about everything there is to be worried about. Who needs that shit?

The Difference Between Planning with a Theme and a Cool Idea for a Party

When asked about throwing a punk shui party, Norman Gosney admitted he's a little more formal than typical punk shui because he likes themes. But his "themes" aren't the control-freak kind—he likes to transform spaces into giant art projects. His parties are a good example of throwing parties in a big-ass way. Known for this flare for transforming spaces, one of the most recent parties he designed was for the Google Christmas party. He transformed a giant nightclub into a "time machine." The doors were made to resemble hatches with flashing lights, and brought guests into a chamber of which he says, "When you came out, it was a century before, and I built booths with

'Victorian computers,' which were people with books and you asked them a question and they'd look it up for you."

Norman uses a photographic technique that involves putting images on slides and projecting them onto sheets of foam core. He then cuts around the projected image, which is lightweight and can be hung from the ceiling. "It's very cheap and very punk, but until you get right up close it looks like a giant object. I did bogus flying machines of the time. Essentially, I did Google circa 1903." That's what I call getting creative.

Norman has a killer pad, of course, and sometimes he invites a few fire-eaters to his parties. Also, once a month during the winter months, he has an indoor salon where everyone has to perform something. "Even if it's just taking their trousers down and reading the phone book. I have a lot of professionals that work for me, but it's always the amateurs that fucking blow us away."

What's wrong with nightlife and the typical party or club today? Norman says a lot is wrong. It's all centered around "vapid models who used to serve as eye candy...one of my claims to fame is that I can still pull together some people who can entertain and be very interesting to talk to." When faced with following the pack, Norman offers, "I consider myself a rock in the stream—the stream's absolutely going to go on, but I'm fucking not moving."

Well said.

Holiday Soapbox

Are you hosting or celebrating a holiday and don't want to go through the traditional BS? Are you sick of going into stores and seeing cardboard Santas and chocolate bunnies three months before the actual holiday? It's not a secret that holidays were created to sell crap. Commercial holidays, like Christmas and Valentine's Day, are celebrated even more because of retailers' encouragement. Think for a minute: Can you believe we are motivated to stop what we're doing, follow protocol, and begin celebrating a holiday because the government and banks and large retailers encourage us to do so? We are asked to decorate our homes with stuff they say we must buy for the fake holiday. When you walk into a store in September and you see Christmas decorations displayed and you think to yourself, "I really should begin my shopping now to get it done early," you are a freaking slave to consumerism.

Valentine's Day—the entire effing holiday—has been turned into an occasion for purchasing consumer goods for your partner/lover/momentary hookup—and to make matters worse, women get angry when you don't abide by the consumer-based BS. Now, that's messed up. The scariest part is that most people (in my world) know this, acknowledge it, and still fall into this obnoxious consumer trap.

If you do exactly as the commercials ask you to, you need to take a look at why. I advocate partying for no reason in particular, not because They tell you to. Have some dignity.

Create Rather Than Consume

Sometimes during Christmas I decorate, but with no traditional decorations. I might make a new sculpture or paint a different kind of mural on my wall. I enjoy celebrating—I just don't enjoy doing it like everyone else. And certainly not like the retailers want me to. Around Christmas (or any other time you feel it's appropriate), make gifts for people. I know this sounds like a cookie-cutter magazine idea, but try to be more of a creator and less of a consumer. It's not hard, it's much cheaper, and if the people you're giving to don't like it, then they probably don't deserve a gift from you. Make up a holiday if you feel they all suck. Most of them do.

Punk It Further: What's a Party?

Why do we even have parties? Is it because we are inherently lonely people? Is it because we are bored with everyday life? Is it because we want to meet the love of our lives? Is it because we want to be surrounded by people so we don't have to think about our lives? Maybe we just want an excuse to do drugs.

Whatever the reason, it's not a clean-cut, simple one for any person, nor is it the same for everyone. What are your reasons? Think for a moment. If it's because you don't want to be alone, or because you're desperately bored, maybe you need to change the way you live. A wise man once said, "He who is bored is usually bored with himself." Maybe you need to have a party with yourself, and no other distractions. It's always great to party with yourself. I'm not talking about setting up your stuffed animals and having a tea party, I'm talking about figuring out how to enjoy yourself, by yourself. Get a bottle of wine and toast yourself as you create something. Anything goes because it's just you. I know it sounds a little vain, but I find it fun. Once you get used to it, you won't even want to go to a party with other people.

11

Punk Shui Geography

Everywhere

Punk shui can be anywhere and everywhere, whether you live in the city, country, suburbs, your mom's house (you poor bastard), your friend's couch, or a hole in the ground (I actually know someone who prefers to live the hobbit life). The point is that a punk shui outlook comes from you, not from the place. It's a state of mind, a lifestyle, and in general, a way of putting your energy into the en-

vironment. It doesn't matter what the environment is, because the practice doesn't even need an environment. It can be the way you react to someone, the way you create art, or the way you create your space. The to-hell-with-the-rules attitude can be applied to all aspects of your life. You can practice nonconformity, creativity through chaos, and ignoring rules everywhere, in any geographical location.

Chaos is everywhere, in any geographic location. If you want to wage war with chaos in your home and follow a practice like feng shui, or try to be a fucking Martha Stewart, you are ultimately living in a dream, and fighting a losing battle. The minute you interact with life, you encounter chaos.

While I say you can use punk shui anywhere to embrace the innate chaos in life, I also think there is a beauty about each type of location and the way punk shui either coincides or clashes with the environment. With punk shui, you can create continuity, or stark contrast, between your home and outside-the-home realities.

Punk shui can be at extreme and subtle levels. Basically we're looking for anything that would disturb someone with OCD (basically punk shui's Antichrist). Wherever you are, you can use anyone you know who has OCD as a punk shui meter.

City Shui

Let's begin with the kind of energy we find in the city. If you live in a

210   Punk Shui

big city, you know this: something crazy is bound to happen when you put millions of people in small cubes (for living and working), stack them on top of each other, and inject them with whatever provincial indiosyncratic philosophies are native to a place. The nature of a city is extremely punk shui. We'll refer to New York as the quintessential city. Call it egotistical, since I live there, but it's true. New York has millions of unintentional punk shui characteristics and punk ch'i. The crazy people who ask you for change on the street and in the subway accost your space all the time; the dirt living in every crevice throughout the concrete canyons blows in your eyes when a nasty, chilled wind whips up; the lack of hostile eye contact that permeates your every step because each and every person is struggling to keep some semblance of personal space as they pick their way through the throngs of people: these are the basic rhythms we face every day in the city.

Embracing that chaos is a hell of a lot easier than thinking you can escape it. Even engaging someone is surrounded by strange paranoid energy. As my friend Speed Levitch says in his book *Speedology*, "In SoHo, to be governed by the fear of engaging others is to be cool. To overcome the fear of engaging others is not cool."

There are geographic elements within New York that can be considered punk shui. Noticing these types of things helps you embrace the punk shui reality of a specific location like New York. In his book, Speed talks about the significance of how New York is organized, and points out some of the outstanding elements that lack conformity. Structurally, most of New York's streets are on a grid. The grid of New York, especially Manhattan, is completely conformist. It was carefully laid out and built for order by real-estate speculators. Avenues run up and down, streets run east and west. On even-numbered streets the traffic goes east and on odd-numbered streets it goes west. Even-numbered avenues on the East Side go downtown and odd-numbered ones go uptown, and the opposite is true of the West Side. A network of conformity attempts to harness and control the energy, but the city itself is constantly assaulted by nonconformists who are attracted to the chaos of New York and who feed on the energy. Despite the almighty grid, controlling the energy of New York is impossible.

Broadway is a great example of geographical punk shui element. As Speed says, "Broadway is the path that follows its own path." Out of the noncomformity of B'way, you get good things and you get bad things, and they are all welcome. Broadway was there before the grid; it was a footpath, a carriageway, a dirt road, and finally an avenue. Broadway cuts through the city diagonally, disregarding the grid, as it embraces the inevitable hectic and vigorous action that endlessly dominates the streets of the city. It begins on the northwest side of Manhattan and ends in the southeast. It's determined diagonal chaos created unique hubs of activity like Times Square, the Flatiron Building, and Herald Square, to name a few. New York would not be New York without Broadway, and basically Broadway is New York, serving as a nonconformist knife cutting through the city. Many New Yorkers worship the defiant energy that surges through streets like Broadway. Becoming aware of how our locations induce our aesthetics is significant as we evaluate how we will mesh with or rebel against them. Whether you're in New York or not, you can use this hubbub of chaotic ch'i as inspiration when you find yourself conforming too often or too much. Ask yourself, what's your Broadway and how does it fit in with your personal design?

People have been dealing with shoebox-sized apartments in New York for quite some time. Some have figured out that punk shui can help either transform space or damage it. I had one client who

lived in a studio and had a futon that he used as a couch. When he
had a date over and it was time to turn down the lights, he pulled out
the pin of the futon to lay it back and said, "Well, you're in the bedroom now."

New Yorkers have long tried to manage the rage they feel at having all of their possessions crammed into one tiny space and having their kitchen in their living room, their living room in the bedroom, and...well, you get the idea. And of course if you live in another dense city, or just a very small room wherever, you understand. Pulling of hair, gnashing of teeth, and drinking oneself into a stupor are the most common reactions. Insanity is always a consideration. I propose trying punk shui instead.

By using punk shui, you can begin to unleash that rage in proper ways (mutilating furniture, bashing walls, and doing whatever the hell you want in your apartment). This will allow your state of being to be much more balanced (or unbalanced, if you prefer.) If you try to escape the crazy energy of the city, it will hunt you down.

For urban dwellers, as we've said before, don't try to make your place a refuge, but a temple of worship into which you can call the urban energy.

Most New Yorkers to deal with their space by cramming all of their possessions into one place. As Brian Ermanski, a painter in New York, says, "My apartment's pretty small, twelve by twelve, and it becomes a storage space and a place to sleep because I'm addicted to the energy outside and I can't stand being inside cooped up, like a bird

in a cage."

As for why he stays in New York and forces himself to deal with the limited space, Brian said, "The New York experience is a like a drug...I love the energy." Even if people have limited living space, they put up with it because they love the feel of the city. The grit and speed of life lull them into an addiction that speaks to their love of the erratic atmosphere, ultimately giving them unlimited freedom in a world of concrete and limited space.

Brad Warner has always lived in urban areas like Tokyo, Los Angeles, and Chicago. He makes the point that lack of space or discontent is less about the place than the state of mind: "In Tokyo your space is always very limited...I've never really felt constricted, though. Wherever I am, I try to adjust accordingly. Feeling constricted is what happens when you are here but you wish you were over there, somewhere else. Long live the survival of those who dwell in shoeboxes."

Nature in Punk Shui

Art and music mirrors nature in a lot of ways. Nature's a lot about resonances and cycles and rhythms. Nature has no ethics or morality.
—Mike Watt

If you live in the country, punk shui is still completely applicable. In more-natural settings, punk shui can take different forms, and you can do designs that are totally out of the question in a city. Punk shui outside the city has a variety of different options and a whole new advantage is factored in—more space. While the clichéd punk aesthetic has a very gritty, urban feel about it, as Watt says, it shares with nature a lack of rules or ethical agenda. Predators, animal instincts, natural disasters, earthquakes, volcano eruptions, and storms unleash energy that is uniquely beyond our control, beyond any sense of reason, and very often inflicts destruction that is hard for us to comprehend. There is something horrifically beautiful about nature's wrath (of course we call it wrath, when it just is what it is, not capable of real human emotion). Don't worry, I'm not going to start hugging tress and wearing hemp drawstring pants, but in my designs and experience, nature inspires the aesthetics behind some of my punk shui work. The contrasts in abrupt or destructive design can be abrasive in different ways, compared to urban design. I enjoy designing in New York, and then moving out to my place in Tennessee and experiencing a whole different atmosphere. The two experiences, side by side, are a punk shui exercise in and of themselves.

Those who worship nature also worship chaotic forces beyond their control and love the disorder and lack of reason and sense that follows nature in its very essence. Even if you're just looking for a complete contrast to the urban and suburban settings that so many of us are accustomed to wasting away in—nature can remove you totally from the madness of a bullshit commute, a pissy roommate, a nagging boss, or a stinking, nasty, packed subway car, and take you to a totally different state of consciousness. When we're in nature, suddenly everything we've created in the rat-race reality of America feels a bit more artificial and ridiculous.

Embracing nature in design can be done by those who live in a more natural community or by those who live in the 'burbs or in a

city. I had a client named Trey who lived in Brooklyn and missed the greenery that he was used to where he grew up, in Tennessee. We decided to overwhelm his living room with plants, trees, and flowers; most were alive, some were silk. We made it so cluttered with vines, leaves, and flowers that if you were sitting on the couch you had an obscured view of the person sitting across from you, only a few feet away. You felt like you were walking into a nursery. Trey said after a week or so, "I love it in my living room and I'm starting to do it in my bedroom. I live in a rough neighborhood, and when I leave my house there are screeching cars, screeching people, gray concrete, buildings, and metal, and when I come home it's another world."

I've had a few clients put a tree trunk through the middle of their room. Besides just being a huge obstacle to walk over, it also can begin to decay and leave all sorts of bugs and nasty creatures to crawl over you at night.

I also have clients who live in rural communities and cultivate a design focus that works on making the interior as natural as the exterior. By "natural," I don't mean that everything is made of organic cotton or hemp. I mean they use elements of real nature in their design. For example, I have a client named Alvin who is really into roadkill art. He lives in rural Tennessee, so there are a lot of highways that go through forests, and he has plenty to work with. He makes bags out of dead raccoons, and rugs out of dead deer hides. Rather than going hunting, he collects the remains of dead animals after they've been smashed by an oncoming car, and transforms the carcasses into art.

The most interesting part about all of this is that he has taken the collision between wildlife and mankind and preserved it through making art that is semifunctional. This places Alvin in the punk shui hall of fame.

Alvin has also carved quite a bit of furniture out of wood. He has a technique of carving that relies on the way a piece of wood has grown. For example, he follows the grain of the wood and incorporates the knots within the wood into his design, rather than tossing a piece of wood because it has what has traditionally been considered an imperfection. He has a cabin in the woods that houses a huge collection of these pieces, as well as hand-carved blinds that have a really nice imperfect lack of flatness about them.

The endless ways to make a creative aesthetic based on your environment are worth figuring out. They are often what makes your design unique. Do your have a certain local aesthetic you can use in your punk shui design? It doesn't have to be in earnest, it can be done your way.

The 'Burb Shui

If you live in the suburbs, you've got a lot of material at your fingertips. The mere sameness that is inherent in these kinds of communities can be useful when you're trying to create a punk shui home. Imagine…at the end of a long row of houses designed by the same person, built by the same company and painted in the same shade, regardless of color, there is a cul-de-sac that hosts a whole seemingly different dweller. Inside, Laura Ashley knock-off furniture is turned upside down, the old local diner's sign is hung from the cathedral ceiling, crookedly, on chains, and a Pac-Man video game machine (like the kind that used to be at the local dive) has been disassembled and its pieces are strung on wires throughout the house. The only foods in the kitchen are suburban fare—hot dogs, Wonder Bread, Chef Boyardee, Twinkies, Kool-Aid, and old-fashioned bottles of Coca-Cola. There is Pepsi, too, for the diehard fans. Shag carpeting covers the floors, and the rest of the furniture and appliances seem to be taken from a Goodwill store with inventory that is circa 1950, or from Wal-Mart. An American flag is draped across the couch as a couch cover, and an Elvis poster greets visitors in the entryway. This is the pad of one of my clients, Terra, who wanted a complete punk shui makeover because she was so tired of living in suburbia. I had a consultation with her, and we came to the conclusion that the reason she lived there was because she loved certain things about this life (Wonder Bread, Pac-Man, Elvis) and the cultural connotations of a lot of it, but was tired of the same ol' thing. This is how we punk shui'ed her house out. Now she's stoked.

Paint your shitty subdivision house bright puke green. The neighbors may hate you, but they probably suck anyway.

Surf Shui

I have a special affection for surfing. I've always felt that even though they're a lot more laid back then your typical punk shui enthusiast, and sometimes a little hippie-dippie, on the whole they certainly know how to go their own way, enjoy life, play by their own rules, and define themselves through no other standards then their own. That's punk shui. They also worship nature, they surrender themselves to the chaos of what it has to offer. Every time they venture out on a board, they know that there is a possibility that as they allow themselves to be taken on an unpredictable ride it's not necessarily safe, and they cannot control the outcome (be it a crazy undertow that might hold them underwater for an undetermined amount of time, or a killer ride they'll remember for the rest of their lives). Ultimately they often find themselves in love with the very idea of riding the chaotic energy of the immeasurable ocean that has been here long before us and will be on earth long after us. Dig.

Speaking of surfers, one great punk shui master comes to mind: Raymond Pettibon. (He might not call himself by that title, but I do.) In *Surfer's Journal,* Dan Duane sketched an impression of Pettibon that identified him as a surfer, in a roundabout way, and also as someone who has gone his own way with his art. Pettibon's brother, Greg Ginn, founded the group Black Flag with Henry Rollins in early 1980s. Pettibon did the *Slip It In* album cover that featured a nun wrapping her arm around a hairy male leg. He has pieces with Elvis crucified on the cross, for godsakes. With a look at any Pettibon illustration, you can see immediately that he works in his own reality and no one else's.

When we talked to Pettibon about how his pad is laid out in re-

lation to his work, he told us, "It's cluttered. It has to be, because of efficiency, because I work on many pieces at the same time." He also mentioned the limitations (of money, geography, or space) that sometimes fall on artists: "That's what punk had something to do with, too...the practical situations...you work with what you have, but you get by."

When asked how inspiration works for him, he said of his work, "You can't force it, they [the ideas] just happen." That's a great thing for us to remember when we're designing our pads—inspiration happens in weird ways.

A great surf shui location is Folly Beach, in the incredibly red state of South Carolina. This outcropping is bohemian primarily because of the ocean and the little barrier island that hasn't been taken over by the development wave that so many other islands have experienced. Beach shacks there date back to the 1920s, and the houses have less-than-well-manicured yards. People come there to surf and to be in a place completely different from the surrounding suburban developments. Located on Folly Beach, the Ocean Surf Shop supplies surfers with surfing gear, boards, and a friendly inspiration to anyone who has considered surfing. The owners, Bill and Bettie Sue, have made some

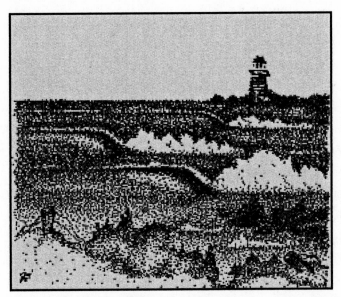
Ink on paper, by Josh Amatore Hughes.

pretty cool punk shui furniture by introducing old surfboards to their next life, that of holding a surfer out of the water, in a chair. "The old boards were sitting around and were going to be thrown away, and I decided to . . . start." He put them together "with whatever materials I have laying around. That's the biggest rule I have, that you have to use trash."

Another surfer, known as Dave the Wave, has punk shui'ed his garage out by making it into a little artist's bungalow. Inside this two-story beach refuge he's made the floor, walls, and ceiling out of wood from old, dilapidated historic homes in Charleston, dating back to the 1800s. To insulate the house, he recycled old denim: "It keeps the heat in just as well or better than nasty insulation." Finding alternative materials that may not be visible is still punk shui'ing. As long as you're bucking the norm, you're doing something admirable in my book (literally).

Punk It Further: Mental Location, Mental Location, Mental Location

Location is not as important as a lot of people make it out to be. As I've said, you can be anywhere and punk shui your pad in countless ways. Getting past the location is what matters. Finding a *mental* location, or lack thereof, is a good way to start. Maybe you live in L.A. but

you want a rustic Appalachian look for your place. Maybe you live in New York and you go for the Buddhist monastery look. Punk shui is about taking you out of your traditional views of where you are and what people think, so if it takes you to another location—so be it. If it takes you to a place that can't be defined by any known location, that's cool, too.

If it takes you out of your digs altogether, into a space that can't be confined by walls, go for it. An example of this is Brian Ermanski, who is known around NYC as the Prince of Elizabeth because he paints outside on the block and lives between Prince and Elizabeth streets. He doesn't need a studio or an apartment; in fact, that kind of environment cramps his style. He finds creativity in the energy of the city streets when he creates art. "Some people use drugs to get out of this world. I use painting to get out of this world. I'm inspired by the energy of the city, good-looking girls, toys, canes, and swords." Who needs a pad, anyway?

For those who want to get out of their space and take some time off—go camping. Even better, go camping by yourself. This is a terrific way to get away from the concept of a structural space altogether. I have one client, Guy, who goes camping by himself and says it really

sets him free. His favorite part is the end of the evening, after he has built his fire, enjoyed it, eaten a little, and then "I urinate on the campfire…it feels as though I'm claiming the forest…camping by yourself is completely different from doing it with other people." To get beyond the mental space of a house and be totally confronted by nature is to go beyond design concepts completely and begin embracing the energy of nature.

12

i.nspiration

Finding Inspiration

We all find our inspiration in different ways, be it politics, music, art in our homes, or even this book. I
think everyone needs it if they're going to create
their own thing. I've said before: you don't need
money, you don't need rules, you don't need taste,
and you don't need to care what anyone thinks. You
do need a fire in your belly to change the way you
live in your abode and design your home and your

life. How you get there is different for everybody.

Creative Space

Remember, when designing your space, ask yourself—does it bring out some type of creative energy in you? Does it make you think in a different way? What speaks to you? Some people loathe organization in their creative space. We all know the cliché about artists, writers, musicians, and other creative folk not being the most organized people in the world.

Some people even go as far as to say that they need things to be a little fucked up when they create. They need some chaos, some different whirling energy, besides a tidy studio or office. I, for one, feel totally suffocated when I see an orderly desk, workspace, or studio. It makes me feel there are no accidents, no imagination, and no original thoughts occurring. To a certain extent, accidents make art. When there is not clutter, chaos, or any accidental clashing, it can get really boring. Boring is not inspiring in anyone's book.

Everyone's inspirational environs are different. For example, Rob

Lanham tells us about where he does his writing:

> If I work in a really sterile place, it's not going to be conducive to what I'm doing. My ideal writing room would contain a mounted deer head, lots of wood paneling, I would wear a smoker's jacket and have a pipe. Given the fact that I work in Brooklyn and don't have space for fantasies like that, it's got to be comfortable and cluttered. If everything was 100 percent in order and clean, I would spend time trying to keep it that way rather than writing. If it's more cluttered, I kick back and focus on the writing.

Cut Out the Filter

Getting in touch with your energy is about living on your terms and cutting out the filter. What's your filter? There are major filters and minor filters. A minor one might be a crappy roommate who has shitty board-game parties while you're trying to record music, or maybe even a neighbor who plays Moby so loud it makes you want to bash in the walls. A major one might be the job you're in and you hate it, but think you need it to "make something of yourself."

Whatever cramps your style, your pure intent toward creativity, your efforts to live the way you want, or your freedom is a filter (job, shitty roommate, boredom, caring what people think). When you remove the filter, you stop faking, you stop pretending, and if you're lucky, maybe you'll become a little bit more authentic.

Authenticity Inspires

Try to remember to be authentic about punk shui'ing your life. After all, it's your life, not anyone else's—different things apply to you than to anyone else, and your tastes won't necessarily have been covered in this book. Keep things in perspective; the clichéd innate need to belong is nothing when compared to the alive feeling you have when you're original.

The seeking of authenticity is what has driven movements like punk for hundreds of years. What is it about the actual idea of rebellion, anarchy, and "no rules" art that makes us want to participate? Some say that punk originated as a response to the lifestyle of the British white society and the American materialism so prevalent in the mid-seventies. Some would say the saturation of kitsch products during the sixties and seventies added to the aesthetic that punk was going for—anti-consumerism, anti-commodification, and basically an overall banality that eroded any feeling of authenticity. Punk rockers sought to respond to this in music.

Andy Warhol's work in the 1960s spoke to the mass media's production of images—everything from cans of Campbell's soup to Marilyn Monroe. Art and music collided when bands like the Velvet Underground roamed in the same circles and began solidifying the movement, which, in the mid-1970s, gave birth to the Sex Pistols and other punk-rock groups.

And why is punk relevant now? Don't we have the same mass immigration toward banality (in fact, it never stopped, did it?) that provokes a similar malaise, and more so because punk has been done and nothing changed. Where are we now? What is our point?

Authenticity. We want some type of authenticity, talent, or interesting piece of something to emerge for ourselves. We want to feel awake and revitalized in knowing we are doing something worth doing. We want to feel as if we have something special to offer this society that we feel is so rapidly going down the drain. It's true, however earnest it might sound. In fact, it's our right. So I would suggest you begin by making that mark in any way you want, whether it's in your pad, in your life choices, or in how you cope with life in general. I can't tell you *how* to do this in a unique way, because that's where you come in. I can only lead you to a different way of thinking. As Brad Warner said in his book *Hardcore Zen,* "Why should you listen to me? Who the hell am I? . . . No one. No one at all."

Even if we want to have authentic impulses, I don't know if that's completely possible. Our intentions are not original, but the art that comes out of them can be. Punk is a trend that has repeated itself in more than a few forms. As my friend the punk enthusiast Si told me, "Punk goes back to the beginning of time, and every day is the dawn of humanity. But every night belongs to the punk rockers."

Traditions of Damaging and Battering

There are some traditions that inspire us, even if we don't know about them. These are traditions that I don't completely despise and I think inevitably lead us to the punk shui aesthetic we have now.

In the 1960s, Gustav Metzger began making what he called "auto-destructive" art because he had some very solid political points to make about man's destructive bullshit. As Metzger put it, "Rockets, nuclear weapons, are auto-destructive. Auto-destructive art demonstrates man's power to accelerate disintegrative processes of nature and to order them…" The very idea of ordering nature, and our attempt to control nature through nuclear programs, assumes that man can and should do so, an attitude that helps two very powerful ideas that bring to explain why civilization as we know it is extremely fucked up. "Auto-destructive art is an attack on capitalist values and the drive to nuclear anniliation." Like all good solid destructive artists, Metzger was influenced by the Dada movement of the early part of the twentieth century, and made some incredible pieces throughout the sixties and seventies.

Metzger was Pete Townshend's art school mentor, and it was he who inspired Townshend's guitar smashing on stage, about which Townshend says, "My adolescent guitar smashing and early nihilistic lyrics returned… to remind me that thirty years ago… I had a chance to build and contribute to a better world." Basically defacing and vandalizing your own art (which is what you do when you smash your guitar after a killer set) is a tradition that makes a statement. Metzger did it. He would rip apart his own artwork. Other rockers have made it a habit; one of the most notable was Jimi Hendrix, who burned his guitar onstage. These artists faced nuclear-age war and corrupt politics. It's not so different now, with terrorism, war, and corrupt politics taking over the headlines every day in America.

So, as I step down from my soapbox, I would remind all those punk shui followers of the punk shui hall-of-famers like Metzger, Warhol, and Pettibon; the punk rockers we worship daily; Alvin the roadkill artist; and so many others who got the blowtorches out before a lot of us were even born. Many of them had a cause and were fighting against the same problems we face today.

I would ask this: What's your cause?

And I would add: You don't even have to have one.

My Version of Jerry Springer's Final Thoughts

I can tell you all sorts of different things to do, and a lot of this stuff is great, but you should take it with a grain of salt. The truth is, we're all just animals. If you look at yourself from outside this planet, you'll see that's true. You'll see the ways we as humans are; everything in society is built on our effort to separate us from animals, whether it's organization, order, morality, aesthetic design, or even language. For example, with language, most curse words are unacceptable to use in public or on television because they are words that relate us to our animalistic functions or instincts in a raw way. Perhaps you'll realize that if you give into your instincts, and reject these accepted rules of behavior, you'll find yourself much more creative, with a much more original life. So I hope I've inspired you to do something differently, and that I've lifted some of the fog of traditionalism. Get creative, try something new, and somewhere along the way you might stumble along some talent you never knew you had. Remember, *you*, not the people around you, create the world you live in. They are visitors in *your* world.

acknowledgments

I'd like to thank Erin Hosier, for being a kick-ass agent and a punk shui extraordinaire; Luke Dempsey, for being the abso-fucking-lute best editor ever; and Lindsey Moore, for keeping all the balls in the air with unwavering enthusiasm. I could not have asked for better a better publishing team.

I'd like to also thank my clients, friends, and co-horts. Norman Gosney helped me get my foot in the door in the design world and showed me the ropes and Jim Budman was an inspiration with his encouragement and guidance. All of my clients and friends who have supported punk shui, namely Hesh Lewis, Speed Levitch, Mike Campbell, Steve Cascarelli, Casey McGraph, Brian Ermanski, Tom Doyle, Jason Meyers, Gage and Lindsey, Zach (Slick) Sullivan, Deegan (Slick) Smith, Mike Watt, Berman, Kyle, Raymond Pettibon, and Zoe.

And finally, thanks to my sister, Amy Hughes, for making this whole shebang possible; my brother, Cris Hughes; and my mom, Judith Amatore, for being the ultimate punk shui master—she taught me everything I know.

about the author

JOSH AMATORE HUGHES was born—believe it or not—in Tennessee (in 1980) but now lives in New York City. A set designer, furniture sculptor, and painter, he is the current principal of a consulting business called Punk Shui Design. While he has done a large amount of consulting for both private residences and businesses in New York, he has also gained international recognition for punk shui.